MW01686483

Katharine Wistar Elkinton

Katharine Wistar Elkinton: The Journey of a Germantown Quaker

Peter W. Elkington

PETER'S PRESS

Revelstoke, British Columbia

Published by Peter's Press
Box 2112, Revelstoke
British Columbia, Canada, V0E 2S0

Phone: (250) 837•3558
E-mail: peter@revelstoke.net

CANADIAN CATALOGUING IN PUBLICATION DATA

Elkington, Peter W., 1923 –
Katharine Wistar Elkinton: The Journey of a Germantown Quaker

Includes bibliographical references.
ISBN: 0–9699944–4–3

Elkinton, Katharine Wistar. 2. Quakers—Biography. I. Title.
BX7795.E43E44   2000   289.6'092   C00–910415–1

CREDITS:

All Photographs from the Elkinton/Elkington Family Collections

Copyediting:
Wayne Magnuson, Prairie House Books, Calgary, Alberta

Foreign Language Copyediting:
Nésida Loyer (French) INTERTEXT Language Services Ltd., Calgary, Alberta
Ruth Schürch-Halas (German) Calgary, Alberta

Interior and Cover Design:
Jeremy Drought, Last Impression Publishing Service, Calgary, Alberta

Printed and bound in Canada by Houghton Boston, Saskatoon, Saskatchewan

Dedication

This book is dedicated to the two women in my life
whom I truly loved
and who returned that love unconditionally.

My Mother, and my true love, Mary.

Acknowledgements

THERE are many people who have helped to bring this book to fruition, to whom I owe a debt of gratitude. Most helpful comments were made by my sister, Theodora E. Waring, and my daughter, Jane E. Wohl. My daughters, Judith E. McDowell and Carol Elkington, added their comments and remembrances of their grandmother. All spoke from a personal point of view, and it helped me to put the book into perspective.

My special friend, Herma Worman, read the manuscript in draft form. Her comments and insight were most valuable.

My special thanks to Wayne Magnuson and Jeremy Drought of Calgary, for their editing, correcting, design and pre-press production. They were able to view the book objectively, as neither of them knew my mother.

To all friends and relations who knew Katharine Elkinton, and who gave of their time and recollections, my sincere thanks.

Photographs appearing in the book are from family collections.

Preface

THIS is a story of life and death, of joy, and of heartache. A story of one person's journey through life.

This is a biography of a multi-talented woman of the twentieth century. Katharine Wistar Elkinton (nee Mason) kept a series of journals from 1905 until her death in 1961. It is from these, primarily, that her biography is written. She grew up in Germantown, a suburb of Philadelphia, in the early 1900s. Her family was of Quaker stock and were members of Germantown Friends Meeting. "Kitty's" early education was in the local Quaker school. School bored her, for she would rather have been free to ride her horse over the countryside than study. When her father bought his first car in 1910, she was the first of the children to learn to drive.

The First World War and her marriage intervened to prevent Kitty from going to college. She could have been an outstanding literary critic or an illustrator of children's books. Her love of books was paramount in her life. Kitty was a champion of women's rights, but not a rabid feminist. She was an entrepreneur, opening the first bookshop in Germantown in the early twenties.

During the First World War, Kitty and her husband undertook relief and reconstruction work in France. In 1938 they were sent to Germany to help those poor, unfortunate people of mixed marriages, who had been caught in the endless and stupid regulations of the Nazi Government.

This is the story of Kitty's life, often told in her own words. Direct quotations from her journals have been used to illustrate her thinking and philosophy. The book can be divided into three parts: her childhood and growing-up years, her happily married life, and finally, the joy she experienced with her grandchildren. The book closes with her death in 1961, shortly after the death of her husband in the summer of 1955.

Peter W. Elkington
Revelstoke, BC
January 2000

A General Note about Language

Historically, Quakers used the plain language because it was the language of the marketplace and not the language of the court. This practice continued well into the twentieth century. My grandparents and parents used the plain language exclusively within the family. The quotations in the book reflect that. The plain language is no longer the language of the marketplace and is thus disappearing. Indeed, it has become almost as exclusive as the court language was in the 1600's.

Contents

- Dedication v
- Acknowledgements vii
- Preface ix
- Family Tree: Katharine (Mason) Wistar Elkinton xiii
- Family Tree: Howard West Elkinton xiv

1 The Garden of Honey Run 1
2 Germantown: A Saturday in May 5
3 Germantown: A Sunday in June 13
4 Germantown, October 1916 19
5 Cornwall, August 1919 25
6 Germantown, 1920–1924 37
7 Germantown, 1925–1927 43
8 Germantown, 1928–1933 49
9 Germantown, 1934–1938 57
10 Europe, 1938 63
11 Berlin, 1938 71
12 Berlin, 1939 79
13 Germantown, 1939–1941 87
14 Philadelphia: The War Years 93
15 Post-War Philadelphia, 1945–1947 99
16 Germantown, 1948–1949 109
17 Germantown, 1950–1954 117
18 The Journey 123

- Afterword 129

Family Tree: Katharine Wist[illegible]r (Mason) Elkinton

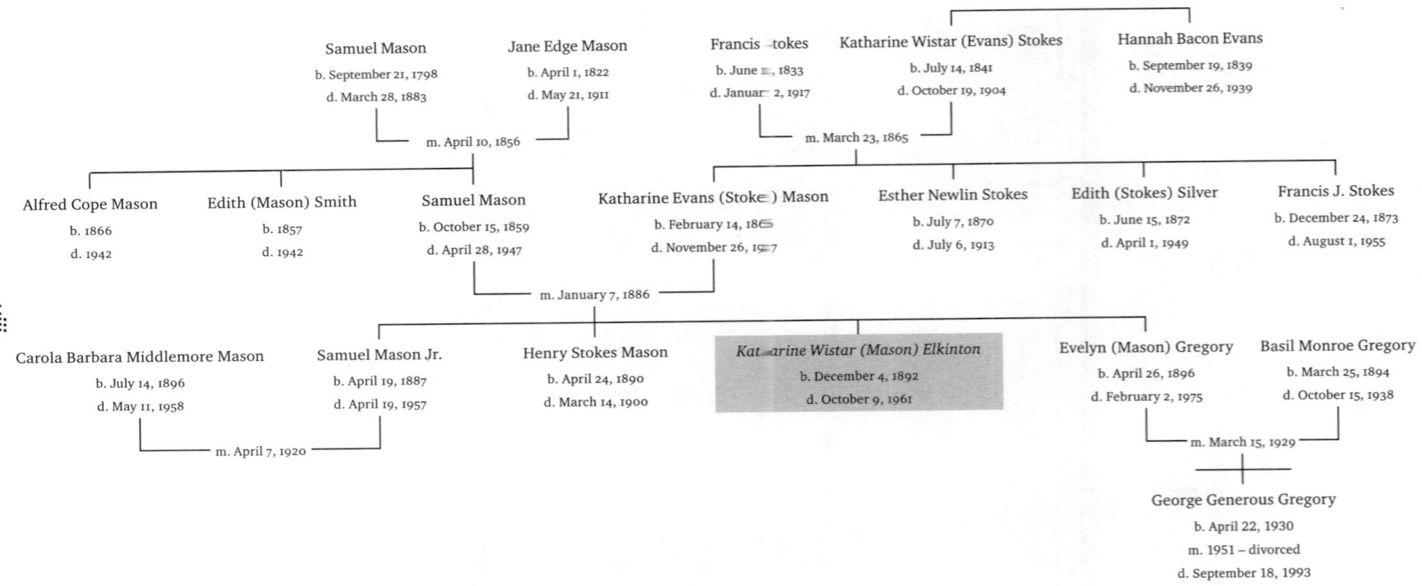

Family Tree: Howard West Elkinton

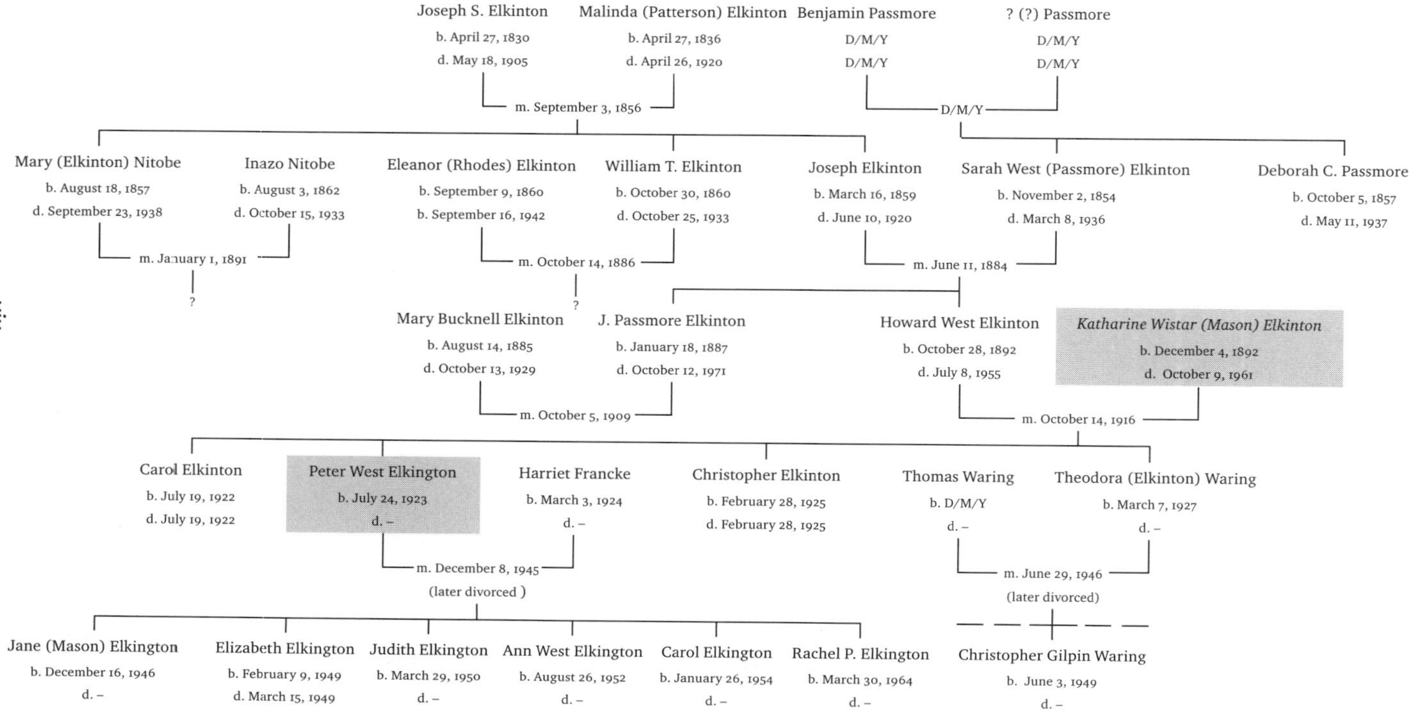

1

The Garden of Honey Run

THE garden was cool that evening; along the back wall stood a row of Lombardy poplars behind which the sun was setting. Kitty and Howard had planted them when they first moved in, to remind them of *la belle France*. They had grown considerably in the interim years. A tree frog sang its evening song. The old gargoyle in the front wall, *Uncle Burbu*, spouted water into the garden pool. By the front wall, the larch tree lent its grace to that aspect of the garden. Noise from the street was muted, but floated over the wall, and yet all was peaceful in the garden. Kitty sat in a garden chair enjoying a last cup of coffee before going inside.

This garden held many memories for her. There had been the corn and tomato patch in the lower corner, but the tulip tree had grown tall overshadowing that area. Six flower beds stretched out in neat rows, each with their complement of annuals, biennials and perennials. As she looked down through the trees, she imagined seeing Howard's Aunt Debby,[1] in her large straw hat and purple dress, her garden basket on the ground next to her. She was stooping, tending the nasturtiums that bordered the garden. Over the years, the garden had become more formal, with neat brick borders and a rose tree at each corner. There was Howard, in his hat and vest, red in the face, sweating profusely, spreading peat moss around his favourite rose trees. Other spectres appeared and disappeared, as players on a stage. The neighbourhood boys played baseball or climbed trees. Her water-sprite daughter was holding the ring sprinkler over her head like a crown. Happy children played with toy cars amongst the trees, in much the same way that she and her sister Evelyn had played with paper dolls and moss houses under the great spreading beech trees at her grandfather's house. The children were long gone, and now only a statue of *Romeo and Juliette*, entwined in each other's arms, remained. It was a most pleasant garden. The cool night breezes stirred the leaves, suggesting that it was indeed time to go inside. She lingered a little longer, pulled her sweater around her shoulders, for it was peaceful here, so full of memories. *Honey Run*[2] had been her home for forty-one years.

Kitty went inside and closed the door, then took her coffee cup to the kitchen, washed it and set it on the rack to dry. She was lonely, as only those who have lost a true love can be. The house sometimes seemed so empty, and she felt lost. At other times, she was buoyed up by the spirits that surrounded her. There were many nights when she was conscious of a presence in the house. She would smile and feel comforted.

As fall approached, Kitty felt compelled to reread her journals. She had kept these continuously since 1905. She had started them on a bet with her father. She often wondered what would become of them when she was gone. Would they interest anyone else? She didn't know. She would give them to her son, for he was more historically minded than the rest. The journals, over the years, told a fascinating story of friends and family, and of places and events, and most importantly, her perspective on life.

She had sorted her journals into three piles. The early ones covered her carefree school years. The second pile, and by far the major portion, was her life with Howard, her true love. The last pile she thought of as growing with grandchildren. While each pile was distinct, as she reread them, Kitty came to see that there was an consistent spiritual foundation: an underlying belief in the power of prayer, of second sight, and prophecy. She smiled to herself as she gathered the journals together, locked the doors and went upstairs to bed. The back bedroom had been theirs since the time they moved in, and it had seen so many things. She loved that room. She had painted the walls with forest scenes. There were deer peering around the trees, or browsing on low bushes. The room had seen the birth of her son, and the death of her beloved husband. She remembered that last night, holding him in her arms, as he sat in the rocking chair.

That night she dreamed. In the dream, she woke with a start and saw the old Gypsy woman of her childhood, standing at the foot of her bed. She was smiling and holding out her hand, as if she was reading Kitty's palm again. She looked up, nodded and then vanished. Kitty woke up. She didn't understand the dream, but she was left with a feeling of comfort and great joy.

The next morning she sat in the wing chair in the dining room, eating her breakfast and drinking her coffee. It was a lovely day. The sun was shining through the windows, reflecting on the goldfish as they swam lazily in the aquarium. It was just such a day, long ago, when her adventures began. The old Gypsy woman had predicted the future and had blessed her. Many of the things predicted had come to pass, often unexpectedly. So she dozed a bit and daydreamed of things gone by: of events forgotten and remembered, of people who had passed her way, many of whom had now journeyed on. She thought of death as merely another phase of life's passing parade.

Tomorrow, she told herself, she would go to Pocono[3] and close the cabin for the winter. There she would walk the narrow roads and wood paths to refresh her spirit. She would listen to the wind in the trees and the soft animal noises of the night. Pocono was her refuge and haven, away from the stresses and demands of the city.

In the last entry of her journal, written as she sat on the porch of the camp at Pocono, Kitty speaks of the old doe browsing on the blueberries in front of the house and of the raccoon family in the woodpile in the back. Kitty speaks of them as friends and as members of the family. She wondered if this time she would see the young buck.

Life had been good, she had been blessed, and she was at peace.

Notes – Chapter 1

1 Howard's spinster aunt, Deborah C. Passmore, lived with Howard and Kitty from 1920–1935.

2 The house on Germantown Avenue was named *Honey Run* after a stream that flowed through Germantown to the Wissahickon River. The stream was actually two blocks away from the house.

3 Pocono refers to their summer cabin, *Hi-Lo Huckleberry*, at Pocono Lake Preserve in the Pocono Mountains. The Mason's built the cabin in 1914 and it remained in the family until 1962.

2

Germantown: A Saturday in May

IT was a beautiful May morning. Kitty was galloping her pony across the fields and through the woods. She rode her grandfather's pony Kismet, a chestnut, with brown flowing mane and tail and a dark brown stripe down the middle of his back. She rode bareback, her hair flying out of its restraining ribbon, her glasses sliding down her nose. She wore a slightly soiled middy blouse. Her worn skirt was above her knees so that she could hold the pony better with her bare legs. She rode over these familiar fields and lanes most every Saturday. This day seemed different; this was a day for a gallop. On she rode, down one shady lane after another and, as she crested a slight rise, there in a little hollow below were Gypsy caravans in a circle. A campfire crackled in the centre, over which a large pot bubbled and steamed. She pulled up, and stared. An old Gypsy woman, dressed in a greasy blouse and brightly coloured skirt, with a bright bandana around her head, was sitting on the caravan steps. She got up walked towards Kitty, took the pony's bridle and told Kitty to get down, saying as she did so, "I've been expecting you." They tethered the pony to the caravan steps and gave it some fresh hay to munch. Kitty and the old Gypsy woman walked to the fire and sat down. Just then there was a sharp whistle. Out of the other caravans poured a troop of dirty children and brightly dressed adults. They were chattering away in a language that Kitty didn't understand. All sat down; plates and spoons were passed around. A woman came from behind another caravan carrying a large tray of freshly baked bread. All those seated around the fire got a chunk of bread, and then sat in silence. The old woman finally picked up a ladle, rapped on the pot, and served the wild rabbit stew.

It was the best stew Kitty had ever eaten. Plates and spoons were gathered up and carried to another part of the camp for washing. The old woman took Kitty's right hand and traced the lines on her palm. She studied the lines for a long time, and at last she said. "You have suffered a great loss and have known pain. You will know loneliness." Then she went on to tell Kitty many things about her life and the future. When at last the old woman had finished her reading, she clasped her hands together, holding Kitty's hand tightly in hers, and they sat in silence. After a few minutes, the old woman raised her hand and traced a mysterious mark on Kitty's forehead, then blessed her with an ancient Romany blessing. Finally, she kissed her on both cheeks and bade her goodbye.

Kitty rode home slowly, pondering all the things that the old Gypsy had told her. The pain of her brother's death swept over her. Her eyes filled with tears and rolled down her cheeks, leaving streaks. The night her brother had died, her father had taken her by the hand into the bedroom, where he lay, pale and cold. She cried out and rushed back to her room, buried her head in her pillow and wept, for she didn't want to believe that her brother was dead. Her favourite brother, Henry,[1] was no more. Later that night, she slipped quietly back into her brother's bedroom and cut off a lock of his hair, wrapped it carefully and put it away with her other secret treasures. This was found many years later, still carefully wrapped, in her bureau at the time of her own death.

Before her brother, death for her had been associated only with old people, or those persons who were very ill. True, her maternal Grandmother Stokes had died, and she hadn't understood why her mother had been so sad. Why had one grandmother died and not the other? Her paternal Grandmother Mason[2] was a good deal older, and deaf. But with her brother's death, now she knew.

The pony seemed to understand, for instead of galloping home, he walked slowly, seeming to take careful steps so as not to upset his rider. Tears streaked Kitty's cheeks and smudged her glasses. The pony stopped in a small grove of trees beside a little stream. Kitty got down, washed her face, blew her nose, wiped her glasses on her blouse, and paused to listen to the wind. It whispered to her and lifted the great burden of sorrow from her soul. Life was good, and even though there was pain and sorrow, God's loving hand stretched over all. The old Gypsy woman had said *Be not afraid or downcast; listen to your heart*. New thoughts came to her mind; thoughts of love and peace. She remembered a poem that her Aunt Edith (Mason) Smith[3] had written and recited when brother Henry was buried on that cold March day.

So still his form—so calmly closed his eyes!
So quietly in death's deep sleep he lies!
Yet dare we think the pure young spirit dies.

Although the veil has fallen on our sight;
And though we may not search these realms of night—
Yet we believe that he has found the light.

My little friend the passing of thy soul
anew hath turned our thoughts toward that high goal
Where love doth reign and hold supreme control.

That kinder love that casteth out all fear
Our Father's love enfolds thee there as here
With naught of earth to dim thy vision clear.

Death was no longer final; it was simply a passing from one life to another.

Kitty remounted Kismet and rode home with a song in her heart. She turned into her grandfather's yard and tied Kismet to the hitching post under the tree. She had just finished brushing him down when her grandfather Francis Stokes came out of the house. He was a small man with pure white hair and beard, and eyes of a brilliant blue, behind rimless glasses. This day, he wore a light tweed suit with a straw hat set at a jaunty angle. He was going to town to make a few purchases for his sister-in-law, Hannah[4]. He saw Kitty and his face broke into a smile, for she was his favourite granddaughter. "Come," he said, "we'll ride together." Kitty struggled into her shoes and stockings, ran the curry comb through her tangled hair and retied her hair ribbon. Chico, Grandfather's other pony, was harnessed to the buggy. They set off at a brisk trot down the street. Grandfather loved to drive fast and kept urging Chico to go faster, but the pony was old and fat; a brisk trot was all he could manage. Down Locust Avenue, across the railroad tracks, and up Church Lane to Main Street. Market Square was filled with gayly covered stalls of local farmers who had come to town to sell their produce. They drove into the livery stable across Main Street. Chico was put in a stall and given some oats. Kitty and Grandfather went in search of the items Aunt Hannah had requested. They walked amongst the tents, talking to the visiting farmers. They found and duly purchased Aunt Hannah's items. Grandfather then slyly suggested that they walk down Main Street to Harkinson's for some ice cream. The

Harkinsons ran a genteel family restaurant, where they made and served excellent ice cream. Kitty and Grandfather finished their treat, walked back to the livery stable, harnessed Chico, and drove home.

As she rode with Grandfather she hugged herself, for it had been a most wonderful, extraordinary day, full of surprises. Grandfather dropped her off at the gate to her house. Her mother was sitting in the large green rocking chair on the front porch, reading. She never really worried about Kitty, since the day she found Kitty sitting on the curb with an Italian road worker, sharing a large garlic and onion sandwich. As Mother Katharine came up to them, the road worker rose, took off his cap and in broken English, apologized, saying that Kitty had come along and sat down beside him, and wanted to know what he had in his lunch bucket. Mother Katharine thanked him for taking care of her wayward daughter, and together they walked home, hand in hand.

Kitty flopped into a rocking chair. It had been a long day.

"Thee's been gone a long time," said Mother. "Has thee had lunch?"

Kitty nodded.

"Now thee better go upstairs and wash up for dinner. Father will be home from the golf club very soon."

Kitty went upstairs, smiling to herself. This was a day to remember. The old Gypsy woman had told her many things, both sad and joyous. She wrote down all that had happened and all the old Gypsy had told her. She put her notes away with her other secret treasures. She washed her face, brushed the tangles out of her hair, and tied it up again with a new ribbon. She changed her blouse and put on a clean skirt, and went downstairs for dinner. The family all gathered in the dining room, Kitty and Evelyn on one side of the oak table and Sam on the other. The young Irish maid served the meal. Saturday dinner was usually a meal of leftovers and tonight it was stew. It was good, but nothing could compare with the wild Gypsy stew she had for lunch.

The next day being Sunday, they all went to Quaker Meeting. When Meeting was over she and Father walked the two blocks to Jane (Edge) Mason's house before coming home for Sunday dinner, while the rest of the family rode home in the buggy. For Kitty, the visit was of mixed joy. Grandmother was a dear, but she was very old, deaf and hard to talk to. They opened the garden gate and went in the front door. This Sunday, Grandmother Mason had not gone to Meeting, because she was just getting over a cold. When they entered the parlour, Grandmother Mason was sitting, as she often did, by the parlour window with her knitting in her lap. She wore a plain brown dress, with a white collar and cuffs; on her head a little white lace cap and, depending on the weather, a shawl over her shoulders. As Kitty came in, she smiled and held out her hands, kissed Kitty gently on the cheek, then said in her quiet voice.

"Now dear, thee may go out and talk to the horses. I'm sure Robert (the coachman) would like to see thee too."

Kitty ran out to the stables, and spent the next half hour happily talking to Robert and brushing and currying the horses. Father called from the back porch, and they walked home.

Kitty lived a well ordered life, except Saturdays, when she rode like the wind, bareback over fields and meadows. On many a Saturday, after her encounter with the Gypsies, she would ride beside streams, or follow the grassy lanes, or gallop wildly through the woods, often stopping at the hollow, where the Gypsy encampment had been. She never saw them again.

The old Gypsy's words would come back to her in quiet moments and she would take heart and listen.

Notes – Chapter 2

[1] Kitty's favourite older brother, Henry Stokes Mason, died of typhoid fever at the age of ten, March 14, 1900.

[2] Jane Edge Mason was Kitty's paternal Grandmother.

[3] Aunt Edith (Mason) Smith was her father's (Samuel Mason's) older sister.

[4] Aunt Hannah Bacon Evans was Kitty's great aunt, her maternal grandmother's sister.

3

Germantown: A Sunday in June

THE Germantown Quaker Meeting House was cool and peaceful. Kitty sat with her family about half way back. She had come home from boarding school for the weekend. She was dressed in her best white middy blouse and a long skirt. Her hair was neatly rolled up in a bun on top of her head. Her summer straw hat was pinned on her head, but at the slightest provocation it threatened to fall off. She could hear the birds singing in the trees outside, and the bees buzzing around the newly -opened flowers. The smell of fresh-cut grass came in through the open doors. All was peaceful and quiet. Her father sat in his usual place on the lower facing benches. Her grandmother Mason, wearing her best bonnet and shawl, sat on the upper facing benches on the women's side, and Grandfather Stokes on the other. The Meeting House was full today, and Kitty's thoughts were floating above the building, reaching toward a feeling of serenity. Commencement at Westtown Boarding School[I] was next week. The end of her school life, what next? She had an uneasy feeling about the future. Her thoughts travelled back over her school career.

She was sitting in one of those screwed-down desks in a stuffy classroom. This was her second year in the upper primary class.

She sat there, trying her best to copy spelling words into her notebook—the ones she had missed in the weekly spelling quiz. The pen splattered ink drops over the page. Her fingers were ink-stained; even her glasses were smudged and, no matter how hard she tried to use her chamois cloth, the results were disastrous. Teacher Emma Roberts, in her stiff black dress and starched collar, stood over her making things worse.

"Kitty, why can't thee learn to write properly and why can't thee learn how to spell."

With that she leaned over and ripped the page from the book.

"Thee'll finish copying these words for home study."

Kitty was furious and turned red with embarrassment. Teacher Emma was so demanding. Last year, Teacher Mary Jones was never so strict or fussy. She felt that she would never learn how to spell. The dismissal bell rang. She packed her books, picked up her coat and went to look for her sister Evelyn.

She and Evelyn walked down Church Lane on their way home. They crossed the tracks. They could hear a train puffing up the hill from Wayne Junction. Another group of kids, on their way home from the local Catholic school, were passing by. Kitty and Evelyn tried to slip around them unnoticed. Taunts flew back and forth from both sides. Flying clods of dirt and horse manure filled the air. One clod hit Evelyn in the back. Kitty, whose temper was just below the boiling point anyway, flew into a rage, turned, charged, and swung her books at one of their assailants. Her books caught him on the side of the head. With a loud howl, the boy and the other tormentors ran off. Kitty and Evelyn, in turn, ran up Locust Avenue towards home. Arriving panting and hot, they recounted their adventures to their Mother. Evelyn was proud of Kitty for acting as she did. Mother was very solemn, and cautioned Kitty about losing her temper. That night, she sat at the table in the living room, her spelling words having been labouriously copied. She vowed to herself that she would show that old Teacher Emma that she could write properly. Every night after that she practiced writing in a clear, careful script. She developed a very distinct hand writing style.

It was a beautiful, bright, clear Monday morning; the sun shone and the sky was blue. Kitty sat in Teacher Fanny Bines class trying to concentrate on the task at hand. Teacher Fanny was reading a very dull story that made little sense. Kitty sat and listened, but her mind was racing over the fields. She felt hemmed in and restricted by school; it was such a bore. She picked up her pencil and wrote the following poem:

A Horse's Fate

Horses are no longer free
but tied in pen and stall.
With checked up neck and bended knee
but by trotting down the hill,
their life is very full of gall.

Now their broken spirits bound
by strong straps into their works…
Crack! the whip comes down,
to remind them not to shirk.

All up and down the margins of her copy book were drawings of horses. Oh, how she wished she could be riding Kismet over the fields! Saturday seemed so far away.

Another year in the intermediate school, she was sitting in Master Walter Cowan's Latin class. He was droning on about

Caesar's conquest of Gaul. Kitty sat there, not caring two hoots about Gaul or how Caesar divided it. All she could remember was "Gaulia in tri parti est." She took out her pencil and wrote a short story of the adventures of a young centurion named Casca. Her thoughts were interrupted when Master Walter asked her a direct question. She didn't answer his question directly, but spoke of Gaul through Casca's eyes. Master Walter smiled, but felt that she should have been paying closer attention. She really couldn't understand why anyone should learn a language that no one used anymore and, after all, Caesar had been killed a long time ago. So much of school had been a bore.

Finally, Commencement Day arrived, and she was standing in the Meeting House reading her senior essay: *Women's Progress through the Centuries.* She had laboured hard over it with Master Harry Domincovich. She read of the accomplishments of the many great women she admired. There was Eleanor of Aquataine of the twelfth century, and her four troublesome sons; Elizabeth I of England, and her struggles with the Spanish; Elizabeth Fry's campaign of the early nineteenth century to bring the gospel of Quakers to the women in prisons; and finally Carrie Nation with her hatchet and her battles for temperance. Each of these women had made a significant contribution to the progress of women through the centuries. They were people to look up to and to admire.

Meeting was over. Friends were greeting each other. She thought of her brother lying in the burying ground, and a feeling of sadness came over her. She heard the quiet voice of the old Gypsy woman telling her to be of good cheer. She walked out of the Meeting House to the grave yard. The purple irises were in full bloom, swaying gently in the breeze. Her mother called, but Kitty said that she would ride home with Grandfather Stokes. They were going to Grandfather's for dinner. She could guess the menu: standing rib roast, roast potatoes and peas, and lovely ice cream for desert. She walked back to the horse sheds, helped Grandfather hitch Chico to the buggy; with Aunt Hannah, they drove home. She wanted to ask Grandfather's advice on what to do, now that school was over, but she hesitated, not knowing how to begin, and said nothing.

Next week, it would all be over. What then? Many of her girlfriends were already engaged, but she did not have a steady boyfriend. The boys of her class were college bound. She didn't know what to do with her life. She felt very lost. There was no direction to her life. She would be twenty in December. Perhaps she would go to work for her brother Sam in his candy factory.[2]

Notes – Chapter 3

[1] *Westtown Boarding School* was a Quaker school founded in 1799 and located near West Chester, Pennsylvania.

[2] Kitty's brother, Samuel Mason Jr., owned and operated the *Wiska Candy Company* in Philadelphia. The *Wiska Candy Co.* operated for several years prior to the First World War.

Katharine Mason, in her senior year of school, 1910–11.

The Germantown Quaker Meeting House,
which Kitty and her family attended.

Kitty went to Germantown Friends School. She graduated in 1911.

Rue de la Mairie, in 1914–18, in the village of Evres (Meuse), in France where Kitty and Howard undertook reconstruction work during the First World War.

Howard stands in front of a row of French *Whippet* tanks, 1914–18.

French trenches, 1914–18.

The stove in the barracks at Evres, on which Kitty cooked the meals for the reconstruction crew, Christmas 1917.

Kitty and Howard Elkinton in Paris, 1918.

An illustration of the Germantown Bookstore, which Kitty operated from 1920–1924.

Samuel Mason Sr., Kitty's father,
and the author as a boy, aged 12, at *Honey Run* in 1935.

4

Germantown, October 1916

THE sun was just creeping over the horizon when Kitty awoke. The air was cool and crisp and the leaves of the chestnut and maple trees along the street had donned their beautiful fall colours. Perhaps, Kitty thought, just for her. She sat up in bed, shook the tangles out of her hair, reached for her glasses and hugged her knees. She looked around the room. It was a plain room, but it had been home for the two sisters. The bookcase overflowed with old familiar titles. The gaslight hung down over the table in the centre of the room, which was covered with drawings, pictures and books. Two white iron beds stood against the wall. Evelyn was still curled up in her bed. She had arrived late last night from college.

This was a momentous day, for tomorrow Kitty would be married and a whole new life would begin. Little thrills ran up and down her spine in anticipation. She was eager and yet a little scared, for she had no idea of the future. What would it be like to be married; to leave her family and live with someone else? She sat on her bed thinking of the last five years. She got up, went down the hall to the bathroom, washed her face and hands, and returned to the bedroom. She sat on the side of the bed, brushing her hair; the more she brushed, the more futile the whole process seemed. Long hair was woman's crowning glory, but to Kitty it was just work. Finally finished, she went over to the bureau and took out her journal, and sat at the table. Evelyn was beginning to stir. She wrote:

> *This seems like a good time for memories to come back; memories of the good times that have been. I very much doubt whether many children have had as carefree and happy a childhood as I. Indeed, long skirts and their responsibilities, brought nothing to me but wrath and tears for lost freedom. However, I soon discovered that the teens weren't so fearful as they were painted to be and, whisper it not among the elect, my responsibilities lay but lightly on the shoulders of Miss Sixteen. School, a name fraught with storms and distress for nearly all my fourteen let-her-slide years, has nevertheless a rather warm spot in my heart, although I don't agree with those who sing of school days as the happiest of their lives. Then one brief, sweet year at Westtown (where I learned for the first time what study really meant) and finally graduation, with all its never-to-be-forgotten thrills, and pangs of separation from everything that meant most to us.*
>
> *Then came the jump from my teens into the twenties, and I must confess it, more tears. I wonder if all girls hated to grow up as much as I did! Since then, the years have passed unbelievably quickly and, here I am, at twenty-three, (far from being grown up yet) about to be married. If it weren't for the dear Squeesics (Howard), I should most certainly turn tail and flee the state, but somehow, when I think of the fearful prospect of chumming with him for a lifetime, my scare takes wings to itself and flies away.... Anyway, if the next twenty years come up to the high-water mark set by the past twenty, they will indeed be happy ones. And, if they fail to do so, I can*

only be thankful for my foundation years of childhood joys, and try to build on them a solid growth of mature life and duty.... This closes Part I of my narrative, finishing a most happy and unforgettable period of my life. May that which opens before me be as full of opportunities that I may be quicker to grasp.

October 13, 1916

The smell of fresh-brewed coffee wafted up the stairs. Evelyn rolled over in her bed, but didn't wake up. She had surprised everyone the night before, by announcing her engagement to a young law student from Baltimore. They both had two more years of college, so marriage was a long way in the future. Kitty put her journal away, pulled on her corset and stockings, which she hated, then her everyday clothes, and went downstairs to breakfast. Father, Mother, and brother Sam were already at the table enjoying their bacon and eggs. Father read aloud from the newspaper. The news from Europe was depressing. The War raged on with no end in sight. Mother interrupted this flow.

"Sam, we've had enough of that. Kitty, today there will be a final rehearsal in the Meeting House at two o'clock this afternoon. Howard and the ushers will be here for luncheon. All of you are to go over to the Meeting House in the car, and then come back here for tea. Howard and the ushers will go home and thee will not see him again until tomorrow. Thee is to spend tonight at Grandfather's. Aunt Hannah has all thy wedding clothes there. The bridesmaids will arrive for luncheon, and then all of you will go to the Meeting House."

Kitty drank her coffee and suddenly felt depressed. The idea of leaving home forever was at hand. But wasn't this what all brides through the ages felt? Leaving the security of their childhood home for the insecurity of a new life with someone else. Kitty gulped down another cup of coffee and left the table. Tears of sorrow and joy stood on her cheeks. She went onto the porch. The old familiar things were all there. She sat in the large green rocking chair and closed her eyes. How had it all begun? In her mind's eye she saw the lake at Pocono. There was a gentle wind blowing across the lake. Little waves were splashing on the shore. She had finished playing tennis and was sitting on the office steps, resting. Around the corner came a tall young man. He was wearing a bright, red-and-white stripped bathing costume. His hair was parted in the middle and he carried a towel over his arm. Kitty had seen him before and thought that he might be interesting to know. The Elkinton family had been a fixture at Pocono Lake for many years. Young Howard came up and sat on the steps beside Kitty. They talked of many things. Suddenly, they realized that it was luncheon time, and both had to hurry back to their respective cabins. They agreed to meet again in the afternoon for a swim. Later, they sat on the dock, alternately swimming and sunning. Kitty had taken off her horrid black stockings and sneakers so she could wiggle her toes in the water.

The Mason's spent the summer either at the seaside or in the Pennsylvania mountains, to escape the heat and humidity of Philadelphia. They had been persuaded by other Quaker families, the Elkintons in particular, to try Pocono Lake. It was a lovely place, with camps around the great blue lake.

For Kitty, Howard Elkinton had come into her life almost by accident, and for this she was thankful. Howard had decided to spend the summer of his junior year at the lake. His father was travelling and his older brother was working, so Howard was there to help his mother. Many of Kitty's friends announced their engagements, but to Kitty the prospect of matrimony still appalled.

Life was too full of excitement to consider tying oneself down as a wife and housekeeper. She couldn't make up her mind.

> *Oh hang,* she says in her journal, *this being a girl, boys have such a cinch of it. It isn't fair any way you look at it.*

She continues:

> *It has been nearly two years now since that summer day at Pocono, when the problem first came up, and for all the intervening months the question has turned and twisted in my mind, taking first one attitude and then another, each one as hazy as the one before. I wonder if every girl is so put to it, to make up her mind?*

She and Howard spent more and more time together. There were evening paddles on the lake, or they just sat quietly talking. Howard was entering his senior year at Haverford College. Upon graduation, he expected to go and work for his uncle in the family business.[I] In September, Kitty joined her brother Sam in his candy business. She was the chief bookkeeper and secretary.

Two cars drew up to the curb and Howard, with the ushers and the bridesmaids, tumbled out and ran up the path. Kitty hadn't realized that the time had gone so fast, and was all afluster. Mother called from inside the house that lunch was ready. After lunch, they all piled into the cars again and drove to the Quaker Meeting House. The Meeting House was warm and inviting. As Kitty and Howard stood together, she was filled with a great feeling of joy. Tears sparkled in her eyes, for tomorrow she and Howard would be married, and she would leave home forever. Oh, momentous day!

Notes – Chapter 4

[1] The Elkinton family owned and operated the *Philadelphia Quartz Company* (PQ Co.), makers of glass and silica.

5

Cornwall, August 1919

TIMELESS waves washed up against the rugged cliffs of Cornwall. Long ago, the wreckers had walked these cliffs luring unsuspecting ships and many a crew to their deaths. A gentle breeze blew over the moors. The remnants of a basket lunch were spread out on the grass. Kitty and Howard sat looking out over the ocean, dreaming of home. Kitty had taken off her shoes and stockings, and wiggled her toes in the grass. Her hair, doing its best to come lose from its restraining pins, blew around her face. Howard had taken off his coat and tie. They didn't say much, but sat holding hands, and wondered when they would sail for home. The war was over. Their work in France was done. They had bid a sad and tearful farewell to their friends and the town of Evres (Meuse),[1] their home for the past year and a half. It had been a memorable and exciting time. What adventures they had experienced in three years of married life.

What had started out as the life of an everyday married couple in the suburbs, had changed so dramatically with their coming to Europe. Now they didn't know which direction their life would take. They only knew it would be different. They lay in the sunshine and dreamed.

The United States had declared war in the spring of 1917. Kitty, with her love for all living things, urged Howard to listen to his conscience and stand for peace. She had written in her journal:

My whole being revolts at this tearing apart of ties that unite our lives, and it is very hard to think that this separation might be forever. But I have not the courage to look further ahead than the immediate future; the way is so dark, and life so hard to understand.

Howard, torn between his family's ultra-conservative Quaker views (they felt it wrong and even sinful to have anything to do with the war) and his sense of duty, simply could not decide what to do. One day he was ready to join the army, the next he was prepared to go to jail. This vacillating increased over the months.

Kitty took the more moderate view. Surely there was some middle ground. British Friends Service Committee, a Quaker organization, was desperate for help with their relief work in France. Kitty and Howard applied and, with five other young people, were selected to go to France. On June 19, 1917, they sailed for France on a rusty freighter, the SS *Rochambeau*. It was a leaky old ship carrying war supplies to the French. The ship swung south along the coast of Spain to avoid the German U-boats. A ship ahead of them, in the same convoy, had been torpedoed, with all hands lost. Their assignment was to be a two-year commitment, but it didn't matter to Kitty and Howard, for they were together.

In August of 1917, Kitty was assigned to a maternity hospital at Châlons-sur-Marne,[I] and she was none too pleased. Howard was sent to a repair depot at Sermaize-les-Bains,[I] some eight miles away. They had been promised that they would be working together, but the British didn't approve of couples working together. The hospital at Châlons was run by a stiff English matron—with no sense of humour—and starched English nurses, who were not really prepared to accept a lively young American with no hospital training. The early going was difficult. Kitty comments in her journal, that she will stick it out for two months and then apply for a transfer.

Howard rode his motorcycle over to the hospital on the weekends. One particular Saturday night they were late getting back from an evening's entertainment. They crawled very quietly into bed together. The plan was that Howard would leave early in the morning before anyone else was awake. The matron overheard them and came storming into Kitty's room. Kitty pulled the covers over her head and lay very still. The matron berated Howard for presuming to stay in the nurses' wing overnight, never realizing that Kitty was also in the bed. She ordered Howard to get up and leave the hospital at once. With that, she stomped out of the room. The two lovebirds giggled together, and held each other close. At last, Howard got up, dressed, slipped out of the hospital, and rode back to Sermaize-les-Bains.

The next morning Kitty, freshly dressed in a clean uniform, hair neatly combed and pinned, reported for duty. The matron, also in a clean, freshly starched uniform, but looking very sour and severe, lectured Kitty for allowing "that young man" to stay the night. Kitty just giggled to herself. Her true love could visit anytime. The day was brilliant; even the patients remarked upon how cheerful, gay, and helpful Kitty was. She just smiled to herself. Later she wrote:

> *Last night, as I lay tucked snugly in bed and listened to the rumblings of the cannons—even the windows rattle—I could not help thinking how utterly absurd it was to be carrying on*

> *like this. People are at war with one another, yet try at the same time, to encourage the better side of life. Fifteen miles away the cannons are blotting out human beings that are infinitely precious to someone. I think one lesson I will have learned is that of the futility of it all, for what can come of this disaster, but a slow readjustment and the setting back of the clock of progress.*

Howard continued to commute on his motorcycle, much to the disapproval and displeasure of the matron. In September, Kitty was transferred to the town of Bettancourt,[1] just a few miles from Sermaize-les-Bains. Now they could be together more often. Kitty worked with the refugees, particularly the children. The chateau of Bettancourt had been turned into a hospital and a refuge for those poor, unfortunate children from Bar-le-Duc.[1] Again her comments:

> *The blessed Boche are, in cold blood, setting out to wipe Bar-le-Duc off the map. Already over* 100 *houses have been burnt or knocked to bits and their inhabitants killed or scattered. Worst of all is their trick of swooping low over the houses, dropping their bombs and then, as the terrified people rush out, turning their machine guns on them with fearful results. Tonight, we have made up beds for* 35 *small young things and have* 14 *more coming to Bettancourt. Still, this (devastation) is no more than four miles away.*

Kitty's duties were wide and varied, from taking care of the refugee children to teaching school. These tasks she approached with joy and enthusiasm. She and Howard were often together, and that made all the difference.

A new 'équipe'[2] was set up in the little town of Evres. Here, Howard ran a repair shop for the local farmers, who were desperately trying to harvest a crop. The repair shop expanded so the whole of the neighbourhood could be serviced. Kitty became the household manager and cook. This suited her well because she and Howard were really together. One day, the pepper grinder went missing and, although she searched everywhere for it, Kitty never found it. The boys of the équipe had frequently complained that she used too much in the stew. It wasn't until years later that the secret came out; the boys had hidden the pepper in the beehive.

The village folk welcomed them as M et Mme Howette. The winter passed and, with coming of the spring, there were rumours of a major offensive. The guns around Verdun[1] could be heard constantly, both day and night. The ground shook, and the windows rattled.

When American soldiers marched into town, there was great rejoicing. The Allied Forces were preparing to move up to the front. The "doughboys" were delighted to find a fellow American. Kitty and the Army cook had long talks together. He was amazed that she managed to cook such good meals on what was a very small stove. The next night, the troops left for the front. In the morning, when Kitty went out to feed the chickens, she found a 20 lb. bag of flour and a 10 lb. bag of sugar leaning against the side of the barracks. Pinned to them was a recipe for doughnuts. The next day it rained, an ideal day to stay inside and make doughnuts. Everything went well—except for the leak in the roof above the stove. Every so often, a drop of water would splash directly into the hot fat. Kitty, her unruly hair falling in her face, her glasses slipping down her nose, stood holding an umbrella in one hand—to keep the rain from dropping onto the stove—and patiently turned the doughnuts with the other.

The troops had spoken of the possibility of a German offensive that might encircle Evres. This caused much anxiety in the camp. There was a great debate amongst the men. Should they leave or stay? Here Kitty's wise words prevailed. They should stay, because they were not aiding the war in any way, but were helping the people of the area get on with their lives. Any member of the équipe was free to leave, if they wished, but Kitty and Howard would not leave. The guns grew louder and more troops moved up to the front. Rested French and American troops marched up the road and, later on, dirty, mud-spattered and weary, the soldiers stumbled back.

There were similar rumours of a German offensive aimed at Paris. While the German forces advanced throughout the spring and summer, by September they were being driven back. The retreat was on and, by late October, the Allies had succeeded in reoccupying all of northern France and much of Belgium. November 11, 1918, started as any other day. Guns boomed in the distance. The men of the équipe gathered for their lunch. They sat and looked at each other; something was wrong; all was quiet and still. There were no guns! They could hear birds chirping in the trees, and the chickens scratching in the courtyard. There was an eeriness in the air. Coming down the road towards them soldiers marched, whooping and waving their helmets. THE WAR WAS OVER! The Allies had won and an armistice had been signed that morning. The great question on everybody's mind was, Now what? Kitty wrote in her journal:

> *It is too soon to think of the reckoning—but it too must come—and then someone will have to answer for the thousands of young fellows who have lost their lives for nothing. American, French, English, and German youths*

whose lives were thrown away, simply to satisfy the lust for power, the envy of others and the desire for aggression on the part of the rulers of the world. While it is too late to lament over past failings, now is the time to work to prevent the same kind of thing happening again in years to come. The next step should be the League of Nations, the deathblow to armaments, and the ruling of justice and fair play.

The devastation of northern France was almost beyond belief. It would take years to rebuild and start life over again. Many towns would never be rebuilt. Even though the war was over, the reconstruction was vital and would continue for many years to come.

One Sunday, Kitty and Howard packed a lunch and set off on their bicycles northward towards "No Mans Land." Kitty remarks that it is not easy to forget the war. Here—fields criss-crossed with trenches, and there—broken equipment abandoned along the road. One field was full of small tanks standing in rows, as if waiting to roll. One tank had apparently run itself up a tree. They cycled on through one ruined village after another. This was the "No Man's Land" that had been fought over for four years. Presently, they came to a ruined village that had been held by the Germans. The street signs were in German and over the door of one stone hut was the word *Schreibstube* (Writing room).

I could not but wonder how many love letters had been written here by pens that would never write again.

In December, President Woodrow Wilson arrived in Paris to a hero's welcome.

I'm afraid, however, that the President will find it difficult to make a decent and lasting peace as the "nabobs" of France and England have put their heads together to pull off some underhanded mean trick and keep the balance of power in their own hands—the black rascals! And then they talk of their fight to preserve honor, and national integrity, against a race of villains—bah!

Kitty speaks of the joy of Christmas in Evres. There were parties and presents for everyone in the town, from the oldest to the youngest. Some of those dear people had never had a Christmas present before. At the end of the day, of course, Kitty and Howard's thoughts returned to their own home and family.

By March, their work was nearly over and they made plans for the trip home. Howard suggested that he remain behind for an extra three months, while Kitty would go home in June to look for some land on which to build a house. This was such an outrageous suggestion, that Kitty would have none of it. They would both stay the extra three months and then leave together. They entered this relief experience as a unit and as a unit they would finish it.

In April, they took a bicycle trip through the Jura and the Vosges mountains to Lake Geneva. They stopped at an inn called the *Hôtel du Nom de Dieu*. As Kitty wore no wedding ring, the proprietress was very suspicious and only grudgingly gave them a room. Finally, back to Evres for the last time. There was one last day trip, to the battlefields of Verdun. Her words bring the frightfulness and the devastation of the war into perspective.

...We crossed the old drawbridge, and entered through a beautiful gateway, the Verdun of history. On winding through

the narrow cobble-stoned streets, we were pleasantly surprised to find the town alive and bustling. And, better still, the bustle is not due to soldiers, but to real civilians, clad in civilian clothes, going about civilian business, with an eye for comfort and leisure. We could not linger long to admire plump bourgeois and departed via another historic gate across the Meuse, which is broad and deep here, and up a long road toward the heights to the north. Ever since the war of 1870, Verdun has been encircled by ring of tremendous forts, all of which have been garrisoned and well maintained. The French have long-considered the town impregnable and unshakeable. All around, as far as the eye could see, was desolation and despair. The earth, torn and riven, lay like some gigantic quarry. Shell craters merged into shell craters, forming miniature lakes on which the sunshine glinted. The hillsides were riddled with dugouts and gaping holes. Further along the road towards what was left of Fort de Souville, we ate our lunch looking out across miles and miles of blasted country on which not even nature can appear to regain a foothold. Here, there, and everywhere ran the white ribbons of old roads. In 1913, hillsides had been forested with hardwoods and pine. Now nothing, other than an occasional stump, and then never more than three feet high. From Souville, we dipped down into Ravine-les-Morts[3] before climbing again to Fort de Douaumont, around which the most terrifying fighting of the war took place. If the outlook before had been terrible, the view that now lay before us was awe-inspiring. Imagine a desert of tumbled limestone mounds, starkly white in colour and, as though torn from the sunless depths of the earth, everywhere are to be seen crude black crosses—but pitifully few when one realizes the fearful losses that took place here. It is truly an appalling sight. On the map, one reads the names of villages that once huddled at the foot of these hills: Fleury, Vaux, Damloup, Bras, all of them once thrifty, red-roofed centres of activity. Where are they now and where are their people? Of villages not a trace remains, for where once villages stood now yawns a series of craters, mocking all hopes of reconstruction. It is horribly fascinating, this valley of the shadow of death. As day ended, we headed back to greener fields and happier homes.

April 30 was Kitty's last entry from Evres and the French experience. There is a wistful quality to her writing. They had been away from home for two years. Their time together in France had been rich and rewarding. Now it was time for new adventures. They finally left Evres on May 5, not knowing if they would ever return.

At any rate, c'est une belle vie, and one that will long remain with us in song and story. Vive la belle France, Evres and les Evreois!

In July, they arrived in Paris to make final arrangements for their transport home. The Peace Treaty had been signed on June 27, marking the fifth anniversary of the assassination of Arch Duke Franz Ferdinand of Austria. To many, it must have seemed a lifetime ago.

Their only chance of sailing back to the United States meant that they had to go on to England and wait for the next free liner. After much scouring around they found a small flat in St. Mawes,

Cornwall, which they rented. Here, they would wait for over a month for transport home. In her journal, Kitty makes note of four remarkable happenings:

1. *A Hawker airplane's attempted flight from Newfoundland to Ireland. Unsuccessful.*
2. *Lt. Read flew from Rockaway, NY, to the Azores and then on to Calais.*
3. *Col. Alcock was successful in flying from Newfoundland to Ireland.*
4. *The R34 dirigible flew from Scotland to New York and back.*

These events marked the beginning of a whole new era in transportation, which she expected to see come to pass in her lifetime.

A final comment on the Peace Treaty. The Germans scuttled their fleet in Scapa Flow, much to the rage of the French, who were counting on seizing the German warships.

> *The Germans are defeated and the losers should be taught a lesson, but whether it is wise to administer that lesson by stripping Germany of everything she holds dear is a question for much debate. Whether the bitterness engendered in the Germans by the snatching of their colonies, and the robbery of their cables, will be overcome by the food that American Quakers are daily sending, I doubt. The French tremble for their lives, fearing another invasion, and yet they do nothing to prevent it. They say "ah, how we have suffered," forgetting in their suffering, that Germany also lost the flower of her young men.*

Safe in Cornwall, Kitty and Howard sat close together looking westward out to sea, dreaming of home. The timeless waves broke on the cliffs below, the gulls soared and screamed in the blue sky.

Notes – Chapter 5

1 Châlons-sur-Marne, Sermaize-les-Bains, Bar-le-Duc, and Bettancourt are all French towns in the 1914–18 war zone. Evres is a small farming village fifteen miles from Verdun. All were within the constant sound of guns on the battlefield.

2 The équipe refers to a farm equipment repair station, operated by American and British Quakers, which was located in Evres (Meuse).

3 Revine-les-Morts means the "valley of death."

6

Germantown, 1920–1924

A cold wind blew down the street. The leaves had all fallen from the silver maples and the horse chestnuts, though damp, had been swept into little piles ready for burning. The wind huffed and puffed, stirring the topmost dry leaves so that they pirouetted and danced across the yard, only to settle on new piles. There was a merry fire in the den and Kitty sat in a rocking chair, warming her feet. An open book rested on her lap. Her newborn babe was asleep in his basket beside her. A yellow and black blanket covered him, no pink and blue for Kitty. He was a sturdy babe, with curly blond hair and bright blue eyes. How they had welcomed his birth, after the loss of their first born, and life had seemed so low.

The return from France, in 1919, had not been easy. They had to establish new patterns. Kitty found it very hard. Her life seemed to have neither focus or purpose. It was fine for Howard, to go to work every day, but Kitty had nothing to do, and housework bored her. While in France, they had been together as a team, and now their lives were split apart. This split was foreign to her. Friends and family couldn't understand Kitty's distress. There was no one she could talk to. Her mother didn't understand, and told her to rejoice that Howard was out of the house, but this was no answer. Nor did the other young brides of her circle understand. For them, homemaking and child rearing were ends in themselves. Kitty sought something more. The old Gypsy woman of the past had said there would be down times; perhaps this was one.

In her journal, she wrote of the many happenings in her family, and among her relations and friends. Sister Evelyn settled on a farm in Maryland and started the *Tow Path Tea House* on the edge of the Susquehanna River. On a buying trip to New York, she had written to Kitty that she had chosen to have her hair cut short. Kitty comments:

> *Long hair is such a nuisance and it is merely men having always called it our crowning glory that has kept us patiently combing, brushing, and washing for so many centuries. Off with it say I—like short skirts—let us be untrammeled. Free from hair, forever!*

The next day, she went across the street to the local beauty shop and had her hair cut short. She kept a shank of her long hair in her bureau.

She and Howard had bought an old colonial house in Germantown. For the first few years, all their energies had centered on making it a home. A small legacy from Howard's paternal grandmother helped turn the backyard into the *Malinda Garden.*[1] It was Howard's pride and joy.

Books and the written word were an integral part of Kitty's life. She was always reading. It was a rare occasion when she was without a book. Her curiosity was never satisfied. For a number of years, she had dreamed of owning and running a bookstore. With an initial investment of $1,500, The Germantown Bookstore[2] opened. It was set up in the front room of *Honey Run* with a separate entrance from the street. There was a hanging sign over the gate and a display case on the adjacent wall. It was the first bookstore in that part of Philadelphia. From the beginning, it was a great success. In the first year Kitty turned a profit of $700. It had been a good year for sales.

Kitty and Howard's joy knew no bounds, for she became pregnant for the first time. The whole Mason family rejoiced. Their much-anticipated babe was several weeks overdue, and even repeated doses of castor oil and quinine produced no results. Kitty became more and more uncomfortable and depressed as the summer wore on. On a blistering hot day in July the contractions began. Howard rushed Kitty to the hospital, but still the baby didn't come. The heat continued. The labour room was unbearable, and there was hardly any air circulating. A small fan did its best to stir the air, but it was really futile. Finally, on July 19, 1922, Carol was born, only to die in childbirth. This death, unfortunately, was due to the inexperience of the young doctor. Kitty lay exhausted. The shock was tremendous, and devastating to both of them. They were heartbroken. They held each other close and cried bitter tears. Kitty writes:

> *Carol Elkinton was born July 19, 1922, breathed but one short breath, and then returned to Him who sent her. What is it that her coming and going has done for us who loved her so? A little life snuffed out before it had become a reality, before it could fill the place so long awaiting it in our midst, why is it that the void should seem so deep, and the ache so hard to stifle? Surely, she was not taken away because of our apparent carelessness before she came? I cannot think a Heavenly Father would thus wring the hearts of earthly parents. Such*

> *a lesson would be too cruel. But if, because of our loss, we can grow more sensitive, more sympathetic towards the grief of others, then perhaps our little daughter has already proved a blessing.*

All the baby clothes and preparations were put away. They had waited so long only to have this happen. Life was very dark.

The next year was a struggle for both Howard and Kitty, for Kitty was pregnant again. They were worried, and scared. They kept the news quiet as long as they could, for they didn't want to be disappointed and heartbroken again. On July 19, 1923, Kitty wrote in her journal:

> *Carol's birthday—she would have been just one year old today, bless her heart. I don't believe the void left by the departure of such a little one ever is entirely closed, no matter how many more may come.*

Peter West Elkinton was born five days later. She looked down at her son, as he lay in his basket. What would his life be like? Would he grow to be like his father? Would he, as the old Gypsy woman had said, believe in the power of the sight, the power of prayer and the power of prophecy, as she did? These things she pondered in her heart.

The ringing bell announced the arrival of a customer for the bookstore. It jolted Kitty out of her daydream. The Christmas titles were on display. The lady customer couldn't decide and took a long time in choosing a gift book. Finally, she chose two from the Christmas list: *Aria Da Copo* by Edna St. Vincent Millay, and *Bab*

Ballads by W.S. Gilbert. Kitty gift-wrapped them, wished the customer a Merry Christmas and closed the door.

Kitty's attention was divided between the bookstore and her new babe. Which of the two would take precedence? A small cry sent her hurrying back to the den. Peter was awake and kicking and waving his feet. He was a very good and happy baby, except when he was hungry. Kitty picked him up and sat in the rocking chair slowly rocking to and fro.

Notes – Chapter 6

[1] Howard received a legacy from his paternal grandmother Malinda Patterson Elkinton. He used the money to create a garden which he called the *Malinda Garden*.

[2] Kitty operated the *Germantown Bookstore*, the first bookstore in Germantown, out of their house, *Honey Run*, on Germantown Avenue, from 1921–1924.

7

Germantown, 1925–1927

THE sun shone in through the dining room windows. Kitty, hair brushed and glasses sparkling, dressed in a flowered dressing gown and slippers, sat in the wing chair in the corner by the windows. She had a blanket over her knees. It was her first day downstairs and she was enjoying the sun's warmth. This was the first day since the birth of Theodora that she had really felt alive. She longed to go outside and smell the flowers. For three weeks following the Caesarian birth of her daughter, in March, she had been confined to the second floor. The nurse, Miss Livesy, was busy with the household chores. Peter was spending the day with his grandparents. Tomorrow, she would be downstairs all day. In the kitchen, Theodora lay in the violet wicker baby carriage, under the watchful eye of the large black cook, Elly Anderson, who softly crooned old Negro spirituals to the sleeping babe. Kitty dozed and dreamed. The past three years had been dark and tragic, but now the sun seemed brighter.

The bookstore flourished, Peter grew, and Kitty was pregnant again, so it became a question of which took priority, children or the bookstore. After great deliberation, she sold the business just after Christmas 1924.

Her second son, Christopher, was stillborn on February 28, 1925, after 18 hours of very difficult labour.

My precious son, Christopher, was born into this world, dead. His baby strength could not withstand the fight just before they got him through the portals of birth. A baby of 9 lbs, 4 oz, but in transverse position, proved too great a handicap; so now my darling Bud and I have two little representatives awaiting us beyond the grave. Carol and Christopher—bless their hearts—how threefold precious it makes your brother, Peter, left here with us.

Upon the death of her son Christopher, she wrote the following poem, dated February 28, 1925, later found amongst her papers:

Little round head, lies snugly and warm
Safe in thy mother's arms,
Cuddle so closely—sheltered from harm,
Safe in thy mother's arms;
Small fingers cling—little eyes close,
Cheeks with the satiny sheen of a rose,
Safe in thy mother's arms.

Empty those arms that are longing for thee,
Empty the place that is thine,
Only in dreams does thy mother enfold thee,
Only in dreams art thou mine.
Sweet little son, so far yet so near,
Close round my heart cling thy charms,
Some day perhaps thee may really lie, dear
Safe in thy mother's arms.

Christopher was buried next to his sister in the Germantown Friends Meeting burying ground, alongside the grave of their Uncle Henry.

The spring and summer of 1925 were strenuous and stressful and a depressing time for both Kitty and Howard. It began with the loss of a much-wished-for second son and the near crippling of Kitty herself. A severely damaged sciatic nerve rendered her leg almost useless, and partially paralyzed. The birth had also ruptured her bladder. She spent the next year and a half in and out of hospital, for a series of operations. She could no longer run and race as she once had. She wore an iron leg brace, and the prospect seemed permanent. In the summer of 1925, when the hour was darkest, she walked out behind the stables of her parents' house and came upon a mound of beautiful violets. She stood there quietly inhaling the fragile fragrance, when she again heard the voice of the old Gypsy woman. It was a voice that she had not heard for a long time. The message was clear.

Be of good cheer. Your guides are looking out for you. All will be well and you have work to do.

A feeling of peace swept over her. She sank to her knees, wept, and gave thanks. There came into her life a new compassion for others. She could now say, "I understand, for I too have suffered." She grew in maturity and humility. Despite all the discouragement and disappointment, she closed her journal for the year with a quotation of hope from the great Indian philosopher Rabindranath Tagore:

Every child comes with the message that God is not yet discouraged with man.

For Kitty, so used to the active life, the next two years were painful and discouraging. Finally, a third operation repaired her bladder successfully. Through neurotherapy and electric stimulation she slowly regained the use of her leg.

Kitty got pregnant again. Both she and Howard lived in hope and fear, dreading the idea of another baby that they might lose. They chose names, but with little enthusiasm. They made half-hearted plans. It all turned on the baby's birth in March.

Howard, too, was becoming discouraged and depressed with the Elkinton family business, the Philadelphia Quartz Company (PQ Co.). It was a deadening grind with little reward and few prospects. Should he leave and work for either the American Friends Service Committee or some other philanthropic endeavour that would be more rewarding to the spirit? Much time and consultation went into trying to make a decision. His Uncle Will, President of the PQ Co., urged Howard to stay, and made it worthwhile with both a salary increase and a promotion. Nevertheless, it remained a dark time for them both. Kitty could never understand why men should be tied to dull and dreary jobs, which they hated, which were both uninteresting and unrewarding. There should be no reason an individual should be looked upon as a "queer duck" just because he wished to follow his dreams and his real interest in life. Life is too short for such drudgery. She wished again that they could recapture the warm, close feeling of working together, as they had in France. But this would come.

On March 7, 1927, Theodora was born by Caesarian section, and named by Howard as a blessing from God. She had long brown hair, a good chin, blue eyes and a pug nose and, according to her mother, was just as coy as could be.

All these events passed before her eyes as she sat in the sun. Kitty could smile now; a new day was dawning.

A week after her liberation from the second floor, she released the nurse and took charge of her house again. Howard worried, but Kitty just smiled. It had been a long time.

None of this stopped the summer's activities. For two weeks in June, Howard was away visiting company plants and offices around the country. Kitty packed Peter and Dody; they drove to Maryland in grandfather's Buick. A two-week stay with sister Evelyn at her farm, *Red Gate*, was most welcome.

This trip to Maryland marked the last time they crossed over the old Conowingo Bridge on the Susquehanna. It was demolished in November. The Conowingo power dam downstream was completed by the Philadelphia Electric Company in late summer. The sluice gates closed and the water began to rise, changing the Susquehanna valley forever. They had barely returned home when they all trooped to Pocono for a month. Here was peace and quiet. Kitty felt refreshed of spirit as she walked along the wood paths or sat by the lake. The baby would lie sleeping in her violet pram, or be wheeled sedately down to the lake to lie basking in the sun.

For Kitty life was good.

8

Germantown, 1928–1933

IT was a beautiful day in late September. Kitty packed a lunch and a change of clothes for Peter. She put on a summer dress, for the day promised to be warm. Peter was dressed in a clean shirt and white shorts. They hopped onto the trolley and rode to the train station at Wayne Junction. This day was to be an adventure. They caught the Baltimore and Ohio passenger train to Baltimore. The B & O Railroad was celebrating its centennial, with the *Fair of the Iron Horse.*[1] There were parades, bands, and Indians on horseback, all passing in front of the Mount Clare Station. There were beautiful, brightly painted and highly polished steam engines from all over the world, quietly giving off little puffs of steam, as if to say "We're ready to roll any time." Other steam trains were on exhibit in the roundhouse. Kitty and Peter roamed up and down, climbing aboard engines, fancy parlour cars, and sat in the back of a caboose. It was wonderful fun. Historic steam trains puffed by: the *Tom Thumb*, the *John Bull*, the *Dewitt Clinton*, and, from England, the *Flying Scotsman*. The air crackled with steam power. Kitty and Peter sat in the stands and ate their ham sandwiches and drank lemonade from a thermos. After lunch, they wandered through the Indian village in Camden Yards. Kitty remarked upon how disheveled the insides of the teepees appeared to be. Later in the afternoon, hot, tired, and dusty, they boarded the train for home, arriving in good time for a hot bath and then supper. It had been a wonderful day—one that neither would ever forget.

September always marked the beginning of a change. Peter was enrolled in a progressive pre-nursery school with twelve other children—the offspring of relatives and close friends. Kitty and the other mothers took turns helping the teacher. There was some speculation that this decision was merely to get Peter out of the house. He was a boisterous four-year-old, always very busy. Every morning, he would be collected by a neighbouring chauffeur and would grandly ride to school in the back of an open touring car with some of the other children. One day, Peter and a few other boys pushed his cousin Joe under the sandbox and danced around it singing, not letting poor Joe out. Finally the teacher intervened, and rescued him.

Progressive education was a new idea. It allowed children to express themselves rather than be subjected to the rigid, structured education of the Victorian era. To a free spirit like Kitty, this was a blessing. She had hated the rigidity of school and wanted her children to experience the benefits of this new educational philosophy.

For the next two years, life unfolded very smoothly. Kitty's mother's health was a concern, for she would always try to do too much, get overtired, and then her blood pressure would rise dramatically. Sometimes, she would suffer minor heart attacks. These terrified the rest of the family because Kitty's grandmother had severe heart trouble and had died in her early sixties.

Following a year of pre-nursery school, Peter started Kindergarten. It was with much trepidation that Kitty put him on the trolley by himself for the mile ride to school, but he seemed very confident.

About the pending presidential election in 1928,[2] Kitty wrote:

We are torn to bits over the election. Which shall it be? Republican Herbert Hoover, an imperialist, a backer of big armies and navies, a believer in the KKK and a disbeliever in Socialism, or Democrat Alfred E. Smith, a boozer and a believer in booze, an 'up from the streets' sort of man who, nevertheless, knows how to govern. I am torn between conflicting emotions—all of which I believe I should honour. I shall vote for the Prohibition Party and be done with it.

In December she wrote:

Just two weeks before Christmas, Howard was suddenly smitten with acute appendicitis. He came home from the city at six and, by nine, was on the operating table with his appendix (which had an ulcer on it) removed. He had a very comfortable time of it, having no ether after-effects, no gas pains, and no complications of any kind. He enjoyed his nurse, his food, and his surroundings and, I think, he regrets just two things—the fact that he has no other appendix to lose and the bill he had to pay.

One day Peter came home from school with a puzzled expression on his face.

"Mummy, why are all those men standing on the street corners selling apples? They look so cold, and some of them don't even have coats."

It suddenly struck Kitty that poverty was right here on their doorstep. She took her son on her lap and said, "Those men don't have any work, so they sell apples."

"But why don't they have any work? Daddy works."

"Yes, but the places where they used to work are now closed."

"Why are they closed? They never sold apples before. I wanted to buy one, but I didn't have any money. Where do they get the apples?"

"The Government gives the first box to any man who is out of work and, when those are gone, they can use their profits to buy another box."

"If Daddy didn't work would he sell apples too?"

"No, dear, I don't think so."

"What would he do?"

"He would probably find another job."

This conversation didn't seem to satisfy Peter. If the men standing on the corners didn't have any jobs, how could his father find work if he suddenly ended up out of a job?

Kitty pondered how she might better explain the depression to a six-year-old. How could she explain the shabby men coming to the door asking for something to eat? How could she explain that his father didn't like it, and called it freeloading! (Is it freeloading when you are hungry?) How could she explain that there is very little money in the economy, and that one person out of four was without work, and many families were without food? All these thoughts went through Kitty's mind. It just seemed so unfair. The depression, poverty, and hardship had seemed so far away. This was someone else's problem, but there was unrest in the land.

Peter got down and ran off to play, but Kitty sat still for a long time—deep in thought. What would happen if Howard quit his job or was laid off? A few of their friends had lost jobs, and had been forced to drop out of their social circle, ashamed and humiliated. To receive a handout from the Government seemed so degrading. She offered a silent prayer to her Heavenly Father that these things would not happen to them. The old Gypsy woman had said, "Be of good cheer, for all will be well."

All levels of Government were completely unprepared for this massive economic disruption. Old remedies no longer applied, nor worked. There was no welfare to speak of and no help for the destitute or the homeless. Evictions were common for nonpayment of rent. Soup kitchens and breadlines opened. Long lines of hopeless people, mostly male, snaked in the door of these establishments. The degradation of asking for help was crushing to a once-proud people. There was little money. Those who had jobs worried that they could lose them. For those who had work, wages were cut and hours extended, and there was a greater demand for productivity. And yet there was no market for the few goods that were produced.

There were changes in the air. The Depression had deepened. More misery! One in four remained out of work, not only in Philadelphia, but also worldwide. Japan continued its invasion of Manchuria and northern China—their excuse being that they were chasing bandits. India was demanding independence from the UK. Kitty comments on these events in a detached manner, saying that these terrible things were happening and wasn't it just too bad. She appeared to have little or no sympathy for Britain or its empire.

In December of 1932, Adolf Hitler, a spellbinding rabble-rouser and member of the National Socialists German Workers Party—a conservative, anti-labour, anti-Communist, fascist party—was elected as the majority party in the German Reichstag. They were elected on a platform of ending unemployment and restoring Germany to its former greatness. In January of 1933, President Hindenberg appointed Hitler as Chancellor, even though he hated the man. Nobody outside of Germany appeared to take this appointment too seriously. The cartoonist for *The Philadelphia Public Ledger* showed a very small man, with a Chaplin-like mustache and drooping hair, climbing into a very large chair. Kitty commented:

> *Germany has elected Hitler as Chancellor and thus thrown France into a panic, as Hitler's platform was one of death to all enemies. However, he is, in reality, a stuffed shirt and cannot carry out his boasts.*

How wrong she was.

The torchlight parade through the streets of Berlin, celebrating Hitler's election and rise to power, cast ominous shadows, and lights began to go out all over Europe.

Hitler tightened his grip on Germany. Within two months he had imprisoned or killed all of his political opponents. Nazi goons and the secret police burned books in Berlin. Hitler denounced the Treaty of Versailles and set about rearming Germany. He established a vicious, ruthless, anti-Semitic, fascist dictatorship.

The second event was certainly more peaceful. It was the US presidential election and inauguration of Franklin Delano Roosevelt, a Democrat. Much to the disapproval of Howard and her father, Kitty broke with family tradition and voted for the Democrats and Roosevelt. Henceforth, she became a lifelong

Democrat. Roosevelt came to the office full of new ideas on how to end the Depression. He stressed that America had nothing to fear, but fear itself. The people of the United States were tired of the do-nothing, pious administration of the former President, Republican Herbert Hoover. It was time for a change. Government action was needed to end unemployment, and correct the economic situation.

Although nobody had any idea at the time, these two leaders, Hitler and Roosevelt, would eventually become protagonists in a catastrophic world war. It was truly a period of turmoil and change. Old values and traditions were re-evaluated and revised. New solutions and new ideas were tried; some failed, but some were successful. The United States would never be the same again. Unbridled capitalism and the role of the federal government were profoundly changed. The Depression would leave an indelible mark on the soul of the people of the country. For Kitty and her family, the depression had been real, but not a hardship. Howard had a secure job, and they owned their home. Even though Howard had taken a ten percent cut in wages, they remained comfortably well off. Kitty undertook charity work on a voluntary basis to help relieve people's suffering, but this was only a band-aid measure—the consequences of the depression had been far more profound and would linger for many years.

Notes – Chapter 8

1 In 1927, the *Baltimore and Ohio Railroad* celebrated their centennial with a pageant of steam power. Most of the exhibits were located around Mount Claire Station and the Camden Yards in Baltimore.

2 The 1928 presidential election was between Herbert Hoover, a protestant Republican, and Al Smith, a catholic Democrat. Al Smith was a most effective Governor of New York. Unfortunately, religious prejudice played a large part in Hoover's election to the presidency.

55

9

Germantown, 1934–1938

ONE morning, after the children had left for school, Kitty sat in the dining room reading the mail. She was dressed in a spring frock. The sun was shining through the dining room windows. Her glasses reflected the light of the day, and her freshly permed hair surrounded her head like a brown halo. She was halfway through a letter from her sister Evelyn—in which she had outlined the plans for her wedding—when the phone rang.

Kitty got up and went into the den to answer the phone. It was her mother calling to tell her that dear Evelyn had come up from Maryland the previous night and that they were planning to do some shopping. Mother wanted to know whether Kitty would like to join them for lunch at Harkinson's and help plan the wedding? But of course, Kitty replied! She hung up the phone and returned to finish her coffee and the rest of the mail.

Evelyn had surprised the family by announcing her engagement to a young banker from Barbados, Basil Gregory. They were going to be married, settle on Evelyn's farm, *Red Gate*, in Maryland, and raise turkeys. It was a time for rejoicing, for Evelyn had been an "old maid" long enough. Kitty had a small worry: would nephews and nieces still be welcome now that the Evelyn's life had changed?

Kitty sat for awhile. She realized how important her parents were to her and how they had provided the foundation—the security and support—upon which she and Howard had been able to build their own family unit. The welfare of the extended, collective family really took precedence over her own immediate family unit—of her own husband and children. Her mother's precarious health (she suffered from high blood pressure and a weak heart) was a constant concern. Kitty finished her coffee, got up and went to the kitchen. She told the cook that there would be nobody home for lunch, but that she expected to be back before the children came home from school. She went upstairs, washed, brushed her hair, and changed her dress. The morning was spent happily shopping in James S. Jones store for last-minute necessities. Luncheon at Harkinson's was an event. While they were there, several old friends of Kitty's mother came in. They sat around a big table gossiping and chatting. Finally they left, and Kitty stood on the corner waiting for the trolley to take her home. Mother and Evelyn drove back to Locust Avenue. The outing had been a joyous time.

The next week they all drove to Maryland. Eve and Basil were married in the little ivy-covered Episcopal Church in the village of Darlington. Brother Sam was best man, for Basil had no male relatives on hand. His sister had come for the wedding. Kitty was the matron of honour. The church was full of friends and relations. After a simple ceremony they all repaired to Aunt Edith (Stokes) Silver's farm, *Meadow Farm*,[1] for a glorious reception. The next day the happy couple left for their honeymoon in Barbados.

There were storm clouds on the horizon for Kitty's own family. Howard's situation in the Elkinton family business was becoming more and more intolerable. Although he strove to do his best, when the time came for promotions, Howard was overlooked. When a position on the Board of Directors was offered to an outsider, not a family member, he was deeply hurt, but continued to work away at a job he did not particularly enjoy—this was not an appropriate time to tender a resignation. He was also deeply depressed by the death of his mother, even though she had been very ill for many years. The stress of the job and mental conflicts made a nervous breakdown seem inevitable. To make matters worse, he wouldn't talk about the situation with anybody, because he felt that these were his problems and he should be able to work them out for himself. The only time he relaxed was on family vacations. Kitty worried, her heart ached. She could only stand by and offer support when asked, or hold her beloved as he cried in the hollow of the night. She wept inwardly to see him torn apart. Howard slept fitfully, if at all, and lost weight, becoming more and more withdrawn. Kitty urged him to resign, for, as she pointed out, the job was killing him. Howard had a tremendous sense of duty to his family and loyalty to the company. He hated the work, but he felt bound by the responsibility. What would happen if he resigned? Could he find another job? He did have a family to look after, and jobs were scarce.

One morning in early December Howard came down to breakfast. He had just sat down at the table when he burst into tears. He could not face another day at the office. He rushed into the den put his head down on his desk and sobbed. Kitty held him in her arms, tears swelling in her eyes too. The children had never seen their father cry before and were shocked. Kitty came out of the den, and hurried them off to school. Together, Kitty and Howard wrote out his letter of resignation to take effect New Year's Day. The deed was done. Howard slept the rest of the day. The children came home to find their father sitting by the fire reading.

The Board of Directors postponed his resignation and granted Howard a six-month leave of absence with pay, with an option to return. This act of generosity was due to his brother, Passmore, and other family members on the board. A great burden was lifted from Howard's shoulders. During the first month he regained his mental, spiritual, and physical health, and his soul. Kitty rejoiced. Howard and Kitty spent endless hours walking in the woods and talking of the future. They had secret picnics or quiet lunches for two. It was one of the happiest times of Kitty's life. In many ways, it was a second honeymoon. Although the way of the future was not clear, they didn't care. Before they knew it, July would be upon them, and Howard's future employment would have to be dealt with. Howard had always wanted to go and visit his Aunt Mary[2] in Tokyo, so he planned that he would leave in April and return in July. Two days before his departure he had a call from the American Friends Service Committee offering him a job as the Service Committee's representative in Berlin. It was a two-year appointment. This meant taking the whole family to Europe. Here was an opportunity for Kitty and Howard to work together again, perhaps recapturing the spirit of 1917. The situation in Germany had become very dangerous for the Jewish minority. Many wanted to leave the country, but reluctance on the part of the rest of the world to take in these unfortunate people made the situation very difficult, and dangerous.

The next two months were made frantic by their preparations. All manner of things had to be tended to: passports, tickets, visas, vaccinations, and an international license for the car. German lessons for Howard. Kitty contacted the Women's Rest Tours for a list of suitable, inexpensive hotels. They were all good, not luxurious. They rented out the house. There was excitement in the air, but for Kitty there was also the pain of leaving home and family.

In June of 1938 they sailed for Europe on the MV *Georgic*. Their European adventure had begun.

Notes – Chapter 9

[1] *Meadow Farm*, near Darlington, Maryland, belonged to Kitty's aunt, Edith (Stokes) Silver, her mother's sister.

[2] Howard's Aunt Mary had married Inazo Nitobe and they had moved to Tokyo.

10

Europe, 1938

THE fourth of July—what a glorious day upon which to celebrate the US national birthday! The family was driving over the rolling hills of northern France. They crested a hill and pulled into a lay-by for a picnic lunch of crusty French bread, cheese, and lemonade. It was the children's first introduction to good French Camembert cheese. Although the smell was strong, the taste on crusty bread was delicious. They sat in the shade looking down at the road that wound through the valley below. On one side of the road were neat green fields ploughed in a strip pattern, while on the other there were large military cemeteries with row upon row of white crosses—a stark reminder of the Great War that had been fought over these fields, not too many years before. Here and there were patches of scrub trees and bush, surrounded by rusting barbed wire and large red signs saying *Attention: danger mines!* Along the roadside, red poppies and blue cornflowers bloomed. Kitty couldn't help remembering the feelings that had overwhelmed her twenty years before. The scars of that war were disappearing, but the crosses gave testimony to the deaths of thousands of young men. She wrote in her journal a simple sentence: *What a waste!*

A quick visit to the international school in Holland and then back into la belle France. Their route took them through Belgium and Luxembourg, down the valley of the Meuse to Verdun. Nature had covered the devastated landscape with new greenery, hiding the grim reminders of the Great War. The broken forts and the terrible trench with its sixty bayonets sticking out of the ground (*tranchée des baïonettes*[1]), now a shrine, were still there. While the French guides did their best to describe for the tourists what a wonderful victory it had been, Kitty couldn't forget the white craters filled with stinking black water and small black and white crosses that had littered the countryside. Whole villages had been wiped off the face of the map, and had never been rebuilt. The hills of Verdun were a frozen memorial to folly. The remains of thousands of unknown young men now fertilized the plain. Here and there, bits of rusted equipment stood forlorn and forgotten. It was depressing. For Kitty, the memories were still very real.

They drove on to Evres where the welcome was spontaneous and joyous. Word spread like lightening throughout the village. "C'est les Américaines, c'est M et Mme Howett! Ils sont ici." After twenty years, neither of them had been forgotten and all the memories of 1917 flooded back. Although many old friends had died, they were still required to visit every house in the village—for old-times' sake. Finally, thirteen sat down to the table of Camille Caillet, for a typical French farm dinner of many courses: soup, rabbit and mushrooms, wild boar, salad, cheese and crusty bread, et au compliment, strawberries and cream, plus red wine and coffee. Délicieux!

July 14 is the French fete national. By some means, Kitty didn't quite understand how, the local dignitaries of Sermaize-les-Bains learned that "les Américaines" were in town. There was a parade, and a reception at the town hall where Howard gave a very funny speech in French—much to everyone's delight. Champagne flowed freely. A tour of town followed, ending with the playing of *Frère Jacques* on the church bells. All this preceded a delicious dinner at la Source, the local spa.

Afterwards, they drove on to Mussy, where the Tangre family awaited them. The two little Tangre grandsons had decorated the front door with American and French flags in honour of their arrival. Kitty devoured the letters from home. A wave of homesickness swept over her. There would be no more letters until they reached Berlin.

Luxembourg is a country of roses: wild roses grow along the roadsides, and roses of many colours can be seen in the front yards of most houses. Everywhere they went, the air was filled with their delicate perfume. Kitty sat on the battlements of the old medieval castle of Vianden. The view to the west was of Luxembourg and roses, and beyond, toward the horizon, the blue hills of Belgium; to the east was Germany and the unknown. Were all the reports in the newspapers to be believed? Were they still the Boche of old? Tomorrow the family would cross the old stone bridge just below the village, into the Third Reich. She felt very far away from both home and family—and they had only been gone a month. She told herself what a wonderful opportunity this was, but she was homesick. She wiped her eyes, blew her nose, polished her glasses, then rose and slowly made her way down the hill back to the hotel.

The next morning they lingered over breakfast—perhaps unconsciously so, dreading their entry into Germany. At last the car was packed and they were off. They crossed the stone bridge, passed through customs, not without some difficulty, as the

German border guards spoke no English, and drove up the hill into a new world. The drive up the Mosel valley, through old Roman towns, was beautiful. They passed the Porta Negra in Trier. In her mind's eye, Kitty could see the marching Roman legions on parade. Vineyards stretched up and over the hillsides on both sides of the river, and on many of the rocky outcrops, stood the ruins of medieval castles. Their next day trip took them up the Rhein on the tour boat *Kronprinzessin Cecilie*, past the Loreleifels, and on to Bingen and the famous Mäuseturm, where the cruel Bishop Hatto lived, then back to Koblenz for the night. Kitty purchased a book called *The Romance of the Rhein*. After supper, she would choose a story from the book to read out loud: tales of valour, bravery, and treachery. It was quite romantic to imagine the feudal days. The children imagined they could see the knights in armour as they rode up to the castle gates, and hear the trumpet calls… .

They started over the river to Bad Pyrmont,[2] a spa in a very pleasant valley. Germans came here to soak away their aches and pains with mud packs, and drink the horrid sulphur water that bubbled up out of the ground. Howard went on to Berlin for two weeks, leaving Kitty and the children in Bad Pyrmont for the remainder of the month of August. It is surprising how fast you learn a language when you have to. The family usually ate supper on the terrace of a very pleasant restaurant. They could manage the printed German menu, but not the handwritten one in German script. Kitty makes the comment that she wishes the Germans wouldn't refer to pork as "swine flesh." Kitty and the children found a small pension owned by an elderly refugee couple who seemed delighted to rent out a bedroom. The old gentleman would sit very straight, looking out the window toward the park. His close-cropped white hair and stiff mustache gave him a very military look. They had no children and had been forced to flee Russia after the revolution in 1917.

This was a lovely time for Kitty. She could explore to her heart's content. Every day before noon, she and the children would pack a picnic lunch and a book, and either walk or drive to a different part of the surrounding countryside. Usually in the afternoon they swam at the public pool and then went to supper. The only sign of discrimination they saw was a small sign at the pool entrance: Juden unerwünscht (Jews not allowed). Life seemed so peaceful, and orderly. The weather was mild. One day Kitty gathered the children and a couple of their friends and they drove to Hameln, a town on the Weser River. This town is famous for the Pied Piper. It is an old town dating back to the thirteenth century. The city hall on the town square still reflects the glories of the past. The clock in the tower would strike the hour, and beautifully carved figures—first of the Pied Piper and the rats, then of the Pied Piper and the children—marched out one little door and in at another. Kitty felt that the city played a little too heavily on the rats. In every shop window there were rats: baked rats, carved rats, cake rats, paper rats, and even glass rats. A sign at the entrance to a small lane, Judenstrasse, read *Juden sind unser Unglück* which, roughly translated, means: Jews are our misfortune.

Howard returned to Bad Pyrmont for the German Quaker Yearly Meeting. Quakers from all parts of Germany, England, France, and Ireland were there. For the duration of the meeting, the family took their meals at the Meeting House. These were mostly vegetarian and very bland as they consisted mainly of boiled potatoes, cabbage and tasteless custard deserts, called *kompott*, which the Germans found delicious. There was no bread and only cold coffee to drink. Both Peter and Kitty got very hungry and had to slip off to the restaurant for a good meal of meat, vegetables, and a salad.

When the Yearly Meeting was adjourned, the family decided to drive to Berlin. The capital of Germany was festooned with flags and banners. On both sides of the broad avenues—the main thoroughfares—both the red, white and black swastika of Germany, and the red, white, and green tricolour flag of Hungary fluttered in the wind. Hitler was expecting a visit from the ruler of Hungary, Admiral Horthy.[3] It was so different from anything they had known. On the day the Admiral arrived, there were parades of soldiers, Sturm Abteilung troopers (the SA or brown shirts), the Schutz Staffel (SS or the Gestapo) and Labour Service cadets. This was followed by speeches affirming undying friendship, and finally, fireworks. Kitty and the children paid little attention to all this. They visited the famous zoo and the royal palace, which had beautiful floors. There was time for a brief side trip to Frederick the Great's beautiful palace, Sans Souci, in Potsdam—characterized by light, airy rooms with lots of windows. This was a far cry from the gloomy palace in Berlin. Here, Frederick the Great would have likely discussed philosophy and music with his dear friends Voltaire and Mendelssohn.

Kitty was dreading the end of the summer when they would have to be apart from the children who would attend the international school in Holland. She had quite enjoyed these sightseeing trips. The drive back to Holland was uneventful, except for a delightful stop at Petzen for a visit with Pastor Mensching and his family. The local church was dated from the thirteenth century, and very beautiful. In the evening they sat in the cool, dark church and listened to Fritz Mensching play Bach on the organ. It was a delightful visit. Kitty and Howard would always stop there whenever they drove to Holland.

It had been a lovely summer. For Kitty, history had come alive. Surrounded by historic buildings, she found it easier to imagine what life had been like in times past. They crossed the Dutch border and were greeted by a tall man with a full beard. He welcomed them warmly to Holland. She remarks in her journal:

It is strange how much easier the air is to breathe here than ever it was in Germany, where always there is the atmosphere of suspicion and fear that underlies everyday life and events. I was astounded to discover that during the course of just one week in Berlin I had unconsciously acquired a practice of being careful of what I said and even developed a slight 'Deutsche Blick'. Here in Holland, as at home, we are free to say and do as we wish.

She continues:

After seeing them (the children) settled in, my mind is much freer to leave them, knowing that they will be well cared for and contented and will, I'm sure, profit by such a unique experience as they are the first American children to come to this school.

I can't wait to come back for a visit in October. Then we will have to start planning for Christmas.

She shed a few tears as they drove away. What would life in Berlin be like?

Notes – Chapter 10

[1] *Tranchée des baïonnettes* is now a shrine. Sixty soldiers, with bayonets at the ready, were standing in the trench. A German shell fell nearby filling the trench with dirt and mud. All sixty soldiers were killed instantly, leaving only the bayonets sticking up in the air.

[2] Bad Pyrmont is a German spa town. It is built around a warm sulphur spring that is reputed to provide a universal cure for all ailments. Popular within Germany, foreigners also travel to the spa for mud baths and to take the sulphur water.

[3] Prior to the Second World War, Admiral Horthy was the Regent/Dictator of Hungary.

11

Berlin, 1938

It was a very pleasant fall morning. Berlin did not sport the brilliant colours of New England. Large barges loaded with coal headed down the River Spree. Other barges loaded with apples and pineapples slowly made their way upstream. White swans could be seen amongst the sedges and reeds. It was very peaceful. Kitty sat on a park bench overlooking the river. It was cool enough for a sweater. She busied herself by writing in her journal. Letters from home had been read, and there were even a couple of letters from the children. She writes:

> *Just now our work keeps us in Berlin. Each day, Howard interviews numerous poor souls, many of whom hold on to the hope of coming to America; by emigrating, they think they can escape all of their troubles. Some of them he can help. Some of them he can but sympathise with. With a few of them, Howard must be quite short as they only come to see what can be squeezed out of the Quakers. The cases that come into the Büro are varied. Yesterday, a man and his wife came to see Howard. The husband had lost his job, but was still in receipt of a salary. They owned a house, had not been much troubled, and only wished assurance that they were doing the right thing. Another man, with no affidavits and no money,*

> *thought it would be nice if he went to the US on the Russian quota, and would we please get him an affidavit. An elderly couple expressed desire to be united with their daughter in the UK. Although the husband, aged 75 and with no money or position, did not want to leave Germany, neither of them realized that if war indeed breaks out, all Germans in England would either be put in concentration camps, or sent home. Towards the end of the day, another unfortunate couple came to see Howard. Faced with an increasingly common dilemma, the man was free to leave the country, but his Jewish wife faced a mountain of red tape and regulations. Most of the people who came were not Jews, but ordinary Germans.*
>
> *It is a man-size job, and one that fits him (Howard) to a tee, and he daily grows younger and more like his old self, before the dourness of life at 121* [the PQ Co.] *laid such a chilling hand on his spirits. I rejoice to see him so happy. Thus far, the days have been too lovely. They say there is no sunshine in the winter so we must make the most of the sparkling, mild and sunny weather we now enjoy.*

After a hard day interviewing all those who were seeking relief from the growing tension in the country, Kitty and Howard would go and sit on a park bench and watch the traffic and people along Kurfürstendamm. Then they would wander, hand in hand, down Unter den Linden, through the Brandenburger Tor, window-shopping as they made their way to the Heidelberger Hof for supper.

Every day at noon, the Police band practicing in the backyard serenaded the office staff. The secret police headquarters backed onto the Quaker Büro. Later in the fall she wrote:

I have never lived in a period of such great tension as this. Of course, there have been times when things seemed difficult and the way out of dilemmas wasn't always easy to see—like storm clouds which, for a moment, hang very low—but never exactly like these last few weeks. Central Europe dangled by a thread and the scissors of fate seemed hopelessly close. We have made and remade our plans as many times as a new announcement comes out in the press.

The Munich conference came and went. The German press trumpeted the great victory for Hitler and the Reich. Upon Chamberlain's return to England, he proclaimed peace in our time, and held up a piece of paper. Many believed him.

One morning in November, after a leisurely breakfast, Kitty and Howard set out walking to the Quaker Büro, just a few blocks away. What they saw en route was unbelievable, as Kitty describes:

Last night, misfortune struck the nice-looking young German Ambassador to Paris. He died from a bullet fired by a still-younger Jewish Pole who chose this way to express his hatred. On walking to work this morning we were shocked to find every Jewish-owned shop in the city with their windows smashed and stock looted. To walk down Friedrichstrasse gives one the queerest of sensations. To the left and right one saw piles of shattered plate glass, not yet cleaned up by terrified storekeepers. Crowds of (gawking) passersby wearing various expressions of sternness, horror, disgust, amusement, and astonishment, all got peeps at ruined interiors in which fixtures were torn down, stock and boxes scattered, shelves emptied, their contents strewn over the floor, lighting fixtures smashed and, of course, everything breakable—broken. Undoubtedly, what we saw were the results of a preconceived plan. The three synagogues in Berlin were also set on fire and the police apparently did nothing to stop the work of the hoodlums. It looked like the devil's own mess and for one who is accustomed to summoning the police and having law and order respected, I could hardly believe the sight of my own eyes. That this is Berlin, the capital of a civilization as high as Germany once was, is shocking. Nothing has so shaken my belief that things would work out, as has this night's destruction of private property.

This was the infamous "Krystal Nacht"[1] or night of glass. The headlines in the *Berliner Zeitung* claimed that it was the spontaneous uprising of the German people to avenge the shooting of a German diplomat in Paris, but nobody really believed that.

The next day, the Third Reich published plans for the Jewish population. Kitty could only shake her head in disbelief:

The Jews are to be divided into three groups. The young and able-bodied men are to be put into a type of work camp as labour for Reich projects. The second group, consisting of the infirm, old and poor, is to be segregated into poorhouse type barracks, paid for with money taken from the sale of Jewish businesses. The third group, comprised mainly of wealthy Jews, will be placed in a settlement of their own, apart from other Germans, where they must keep themselves going at their own expense. Again it seems unbelievable, and I go about fairly gasping for air at the immensity and crushing finality of these plans. It is indeed like the tread of an enormous juggernaut that rolls relentlessly across a section of helpless humanity and there seems no power to stop it, short of war.

A week later, it was Busstag, a church day of repentance which the authorities certainly didn't celebrate. Kitty writes again with an aching heart:

> *Last Friday morning, through until Sunday night, troops of SA (the brown shirts) went around to Jewish houses and tore the men from their families, often in the most brutal manner. At 5:00 a.m., they burst into bedrooms, hardly allowing the men to dress and herded them off to an unknown destination, leaving terrified women and children at home. In some cases, women were also taken, but so far the vast majority have been men aged 18 to 65. In addition, all Jewish relief organizations have been closed and their records stolen, and the publication of all Jewish newspapers is now forbidden.*

The Quaker Büro was inundated with people who had lost everything and were seeking some modicum of comfort or help. This time, mostly Jews sought the relief of escape. Both Kitty and Howard were hard-pressed, and deeply moved as many people left in tears.

Kitty welcomed the trip to Holland to be with the children for Thanksgiving. What a relief it was to cross into Holland, leaving behind the abnormal, hectic, hunted life for a peaceful happy existence. They celebrated Thanksgiving with a picnic lunch in the *Sahara*, a huge deposit of pure white sand located in the middle of a pine forest—the remnant of an ancient beach from some bygone ocean.

The return to Berlin plunged them once again into the schizophrenic world of Germany. Christmas decorations hung from lampposts. Those store windows not boarded up were decorated and filled with all kinds of Christmas goodies to delight shoppers. Volunteers, dressed in red and white, stood on street corners ringing bells and seeking donations for *Winterhilfe*, the German equivalent of the Salvation Army. Pageants and carols marked the celebration of Christmas. Apparently, Europe was at peace. Behind the facade of cheer and joy, Jews and dissidents were being arrested and sent to concentration camps. Their real property was confiscated, assets seized, and businesses closed. It was unreal. The German people walked around with their eyes closed, seeing only what they wanted to see.

Many times, Kitty would be asked, "Why does the rest of the world hate us? Why does America hate us? We are only trying to live peacefully. Hitler is a great leader, and why doesn't the rest of Europe follow his lead?"

It was not easy to offer any answers to these questions, certainly any that the Germans would understand. Propaganda in the press and over the radio was too strong.

An endless stream of Jews poured through the doors of the Quaker Büro seeking refuge and escape. No Jew was allowed to leave the country with more than 10 marks (US$2.50). Kitty and Howard could only try to offer comfort and reassurance. As for answers, there were none. The rest of the world had closed its doors. Regulations followed by further regulations were constantly issued by the government offices. If the rest of the world would not help Germany with the Jewish problem, then Germany would have to take extreme measures. They never said exactly what these measures were, but the threat was there. Unknown except to the inner circle of the Nazi Party, plans for the Holocaust were well underway.

Christmas was fast approaching. Kitty and Howard picked up the children and drove to Amsterdam. It snowed and the canals were frozen. Rosy-cheeked Dutch citizens skated up and down.

The bells of the *Ould Kerk* sounded brilliant and clear on the frosty air. Amsterdam was such a relief from the drabness of Berlin.

Christmas and New Year were spent at the Hotel Britannic in Paris, the *City of Lights*.

Notes – Chapter 11

[1] *Krystal Nacht*, in November of 1938, was an event where Storm Troopers and the SS systematically destroyed every Jewish-owned store in the country. The raid was an act of revenge after the shooting of a German diplomat in Paris. The German press claimed it to be a righteous uprising of the German people.

12
Berlin, 1939

THEIR return to Berlin was marked by an unpleasant surprise. The hospice where they were staying informed them that rooms would not be available anymore. No reason was given. It turned out later that the Nazi Party had been displeased, and had put the squeeze on the hospice, because they had entertained Jews, and the hospice's clientele didn't like it. Pressure was slowly being put on all foreign agencies that were trying to help the Jews.

Kitty bought a pair of leather breeches for her nephew George Generous Gregory. She writes of the encounter with the post office:

> *This land is a great believer in red tape, yards of it. The other day I wanted to mail a pair of leather breeches to GGG, and started bravely off only to be told by Eva that I must stop at the stationery store and buy the necessary papers. After some explanations, I got this straight, bought my papers and went to the special Post Office, and then my troubles began. A hideous list of questions had to be answered three times over, and all had to be written out in the most abstruse German, with many an underlining and the man in charge shook his head throughout the procedure. As if this were not sufficient, a third triptych had to be made out just to prove this small*

package was not to be sold in the USA. Finally, after I had been home once in a rage, and obtained some further explanations from Eva, yet another form had to be made out and sent to the Reichsminister, just why—I don't know. Never again will I mail anything from this crazy place.... Example #2: we tried to find out the cost of a long distance call to Vienna, but no, the proper bureau was closed and the phone company had no way of finding out. Some system, I call it.

One morning, an invitation arrived from the Reichsminister for them to attend the National Holiday celebration of the German People on the first of May, in the Lust Garden. Hitler would be speaking. Kitty's laundress had told her with pride that "once you saw Hitler, you will never forget him, he is fabelhaft" (wonderful). Later in the week their guide came by and they joined a group of other foreigners, including Americans, in the press seats:

We found the huge grandstands backed by the usual red banners marking off a big open-air auditorium; both stands and grounds were already packed when we got there at 11:30 a.m. At noon, the guard of honour marched down through the crowd and then Hitler himself—and a clever speech he made, starting off with local jokes in Berliner dialect.

The crowd loved it. Cheers filled the stadium. The whole arena echoed with thousands of *Sieg Heils*, as hands were raised in the stiff-armed salute. Kitty looked down the line of spectators and saw, much to her amazement, Howard's hand in the air. She folded her hands and grimly refused to salute. Hitler then launched into a diatribe accusing the Western powers of encircling Germany, threatening to cut off their lifeblood, when all Germany asked of the world was to be recognized as a great power. More cheers, more *Sieg Heils*. This place was rocking, and Hitler had the crowd in the palm of his hand. The afternoon ended with the mass singing of *Deutschland über alles* and the *Horst Wessel Lied*. It was a sight to remember.

Later that night, Kitty chided Howard for saluting. His rather lame answer was that one should do as the Romans do. She felt this was no excuse, and told him so. The political climate was becoming more and more heated. The propaganda mills ground out an endless copy of lies. Now that Czechoslovakia had been dismembered, all attention was focused on Poland. "Ruthless Poles Murder Innocent German Tourists" proclaimed the headline. This intolerable behavior demanded action, but the government policy seemed to be one of restraint. They could afford to be tolerant. The next day, the headlines would again assert that the Germans living in Danzig wanted to join the Fatherland, and foreign powers were preventing them. Its aggressive neighbours were besetting poor, innocent Germany. The situation couldn't last long.

Kitty and Howard lived with the Drs. Gottstein; both were well-respected medical doctors. Their practice had been curtailed by the new anti-Semitic regulations. One night, the Gestapo broke into the house and arrested Dr. Gottstein and bundled him off to a concentration camp. His wife was frantic; six months passed with no word. She realized that Howard couldn't help, because of government regulations. In desperation, she went to Copenhagen to plead her case with the American Consulate. Somehow, she acquired two tickets and visas for the US. These she presented to Howard, who took them to the emigration bureau. Within two days, Dr. Gottstein was released with orders to leave the country within 24 hours. As he and Howard flew to Copenhagen, Dr. Gottstein pointed down. There, in a clearing in the woods, was the infamous Sachsenhausen concentration camp. Dr. Gottstein had often watched the plane from Berlin to Copenhagen fly over, and had wondered would he ever be on it. Kitty comments:

> *Today, I have had a series of married couples to try and place—all of them discouraging cases and almost impossible to get to England. The new restrictions seem to undermine all possibilities that one struggles to think of. When the discouraged applicants ask, 'Well what can I do and where can I go,' (as one did today, when I told her she was too old to train as a midwife or a nurse) one is at one's wits end to advise. Some of the restrictions seem ironic; for example, a woman must be divorced or separated from her husband in order to get a job in England, but if she is divorced she cannot get into the US. No one of the white-collar class is wanted in Australia or New Zealand, no doctors or lawyers can practice in England, but in the US they are more than welcome.*

Restrictions are piled on top of restrictions, and all are bound up with yards of red tape. It was almost impossible for anyone to leave Germany. There were severe currency and property restrictions, particularly for Jews. Ordinary Germans were still free to travel if they had the money. All the time, the final solution to the Jewish problem was going on. There were secret mass arrests, incarcerations, and executions. Nobody knew the full extent of the activities of the Gestapo. Kitty and Howard did their best for those who came to the Büro. It was heart-rending work.

One day, a lady came into the office and asked Kitty if she could find out what had happened to her husband. He was not a Jew, but had been arrested by the always-suspicious Gestapo. That afternoon, Kitty went around the corner to the grim Gestapo

Kitty holding lion cubs at the Berlin Zoo, September 1938.

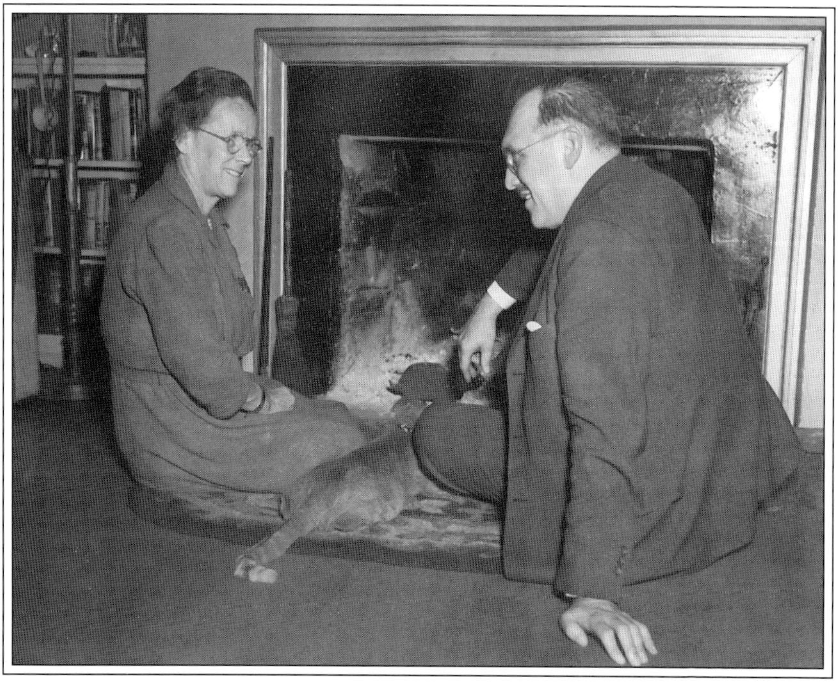

Kitty and Howard relaxing in their home, *Honey Run*, in 1947.
Above, *Bunny* the cat lies between them.

The cabin, *Hi-Lo Huckleberry*, at Pocono lake Preserve, July 1949.
This was Kitty's refuge and retreat.

Kitty's Grandfather's house at 704 Locust Avenue.
The author and his family are seen in the foreground, 1951.

A side view of Kitty's Germantown home, *Honey Run*, showing the three parts of the house, in 1953.

A statue of *Romeo & Juliette* in a grove of trees in the garden of *Honey Run*.

Kitty, pictured in 1956, reading her grandfather's (Samuel Mason) journals from 1838–44.

Samuel Mason Jr., Kitty's older brother, working at his loom, 1956.

One of the last pictures of Kitty, seen here standing on the front steps of *Honey Run*, in 1960.

Katharine Wistar Elkinton in 1954.

headquarters in Alexanderplatz. She marched in though the front door and asked to speak to the commandant. The apple-cheeked young officer on duty was a little taken aback. Here was a small American lady who spoke German, demanding to see the commandant. This was unheard of. He made several hasty phone calls. Kitty was ushered into an adjoining room, and told to wait.

Soon, another young officer, in a crisp black uniform with the bright silver insignia of the Gestapo came in, saluted, and asked what she wanted. She repeated her demand that she wished to speak to the commandant. The young officer frowned, hesitated, and then beckoned her to follow him. Up the stairs they went, down a long hall to a pair of beautiful ornate doors. The young officer knocked, the doors opened silently and Kitty was bowed into the room.

It was a beautiful room. Oil paintings graced the walls, and oriental rugs covered large parts of the floor. Behind a massive, carved oak desk sat the commandant. He rose, gestured Kitty to a chair, ordered coffee and sat down beside her. The coffee was excellent and it was served in beautiful china cups and saucers. In perfect English, the commandant asked who she was and why she had come to see him. The commandant knew full well who she was and where she came from. Kitty told him she was a Quaker from the Büro around the corner, and she wanted to find out about a certain gentleman. She and the commandant chatted for about half an hour. Then he rose, thanked her for coming, and said that she would have an answer the next day.

Kitty walked down the hall, through one set of closed doors after another, down the stairs and through more doors. The duty officer rose, saluted, and bowed to her out the front door. As she walked along the sidewalk, she realized how easily it would been to vanish. She was scared, and shaken. The next day, the young

Gestapo officer came to the Büro with a letter from the commandant. He thanked her for coming, and expressed how much he had enjoyed their visit. The gentleman about whom she had inquired had, unfortunately, become very ill and had passed away. His family had been notified.

The young officer had waited. "Is there an answer," he said?

"No," Kitty replied, "but please convey my thanks to the commandant."

The officer clicked his heels, saluted and left. Kitty sat for a long time. The enormity of the whole situation flooded over her. People could vanish and never be heard of again. Nobody knew what went on in the concentration camps; nobody asked, and nobody seemed to care.

Summer was approaching. The family had planned a vacation in England. Kitty's parents were not in the best of health. So it was decided that she and her daughter would go back to the US for the summer, returning to Europe in September of 1939.

It was very hard to say goodbye to him (Howard) and see him drive off in the Fordy.

What would happen to him, or her son, if war should break out? She hurriedly put these thoughts out of her mind, for it was hard enough to be separated for the summer. She refers to a letter from Howard:

His last letter says things are growing steadily worse in Berlin.

August 18—Today is noteworthy as for the first time since Christopher was born and my foot paralyzed, I played tennis and not too badly.

This was a great accomplishment. It had taken 15 years for her foot and leg to become normal again.

September 3—England formally declared war on Germany after it had attacked Poland, occupied Danzig, and bombed Warschau—and the whole horrible business begins over again.

Cable lines were cut and postal service curtailed. Howard was in Berlin and her son, so she thought, was in Paris, and there was no way she could contact either one. She worried about them both. As the summer of 1939 drew to a close, the world was again at war.

13

Germantown, 1939–1941

THE mist hung in the valleys. It was early dawn and the light on the horizon gave promise of a clear day. A cock crowed and was answered. Cows lowed in the meadow, a dog barked in a farmyard, a wolf answered from a nearby wood. All was still in the early dawn. Silently, the gray-green soldiers moved out of the woods. Trucks, guns, and motorcycles swept down the roads and lanes. From all sides, the German army poured into Poland. The startled Poles had no time to react. Towns, villages, and farms fell before the onslaught. Airfields were bombed and strafed, and the Polish air force, ready for combat, was smashed and destroyed. Within 24 hours, a third of Poland was occupied. The gray-green soldiers and their black uniformed companions moved from hamlet to hamlet brutally crushing any resistance.

Howard sat at his desk in Berlin, depressed. The headlines claimed that the wicked Poles had attacked the Fatherland. The German army, by its prompt action, had prevented a catastrophe. Howard walked along Friedrichstrasse and Unter den Linden, and all he saw was resignation on the faces of the people. There was no cheering, no bands playing, and no parades. The country was at war. Across Europe, in Paris, his son watched the faces of the French; faces of sadness and defeat. There was no appetite for war, but here we go again, and the sirens wailed.

Kitty worried. Her beloved husband was in Berlin, and her precious son in Paris. What would happen to them? Howard received a telegram from Paris saying "Peter failed." What did this mean? Had he failed in his attempt to return to the school in Ommen? Or had something else happened? So many questions. Howard sent a boat ticket to Paris, in case Peter was still there. The ticket was for the *Queen Mary*, but that stately ship sat safely in New York harbour. Kitty wrote:

> *This business of not knowing where my loved ones are or what they are doing is very wearing; knowing anything would be better than living in ignorance. As for my dear Howard, I do not like to think how long it may be till I see him again. The war goes on, Warschau has been bombed and taken, and my guess is that Hitler will now try to make peace with England and France, having gained one of his chief goals. The French on the Maginot Line are attacking, rather mildly, the Siegfried Line near Strasbourg and the British flyers constantly shower the Reich with propaganda leaflets telling them that the war is not against them, but only against Hitler and what he stands for. It is the most amazing development all round...I wish I were there with him, but what can one do under the circumstances, but carry on here.*
>
> *September 10, 1939*

Later that week, her son arrived at the front door, having managed to get himself home, across France to England, and to New York via the Cunard liner SS *Aquatania*.[1] There had been total radio silence from the time that ship sailed from Southampton, until she docked in New York. He had quite a tale to tell.

Yesterday was one of those times when 3,000 miles seems 3,000,000 and one is powerless to do anything, but practice self control; and do it intensively. About 10:00 a.m., Clarence[2] *called me to say they had received a cable from the* Associated Press *saying Howard had been seriously injured in an auto accident on the way to Warschau, with Morris and MacDonald.*[3] *The early afternoon papers put the story on the front page and it was twice mentioned on radio news reports. Luckily, I did not see or hear these notices until the cable arrived, direct from MacDonald, which put my heart back in normal gear again and made the sun shine once more. What a numbing sensation it is to have to wait for news which you feel may prove fatal to all one's hopes; it was a sad few hours. I was awfully afraid he would be taken to a Polish hospital and not get any care, but luckily they were near enough to Berlin to go back there and this morning's cable reports him in the Charitee Krankenhaus with one of the best doctors in Germany in charge. Dear knows my heart is often very heavy—I miss him so much. I realize that I am so fortunate in having my dear one alive even though he is so far away. I am almost afraid to hope that he will be home before too long.*

October 19, 1939

Howard's injuries were more serious than first realized. A broken arm, a broken collarbone, and a pelvis cracked in two or three places. This meant a prolonged stay of four to five weeks in the hospital. Late in November, he was discharged. His nurse escorted him to Genoa and aboard ship. The German Government paid for all expenses. He was still pretty weak when he arrived in New York. Great was Kitty's joy to see him standing at the rail as the ship pulled in. He was home, in time for Christmas too!

But here at Honey Run, *the peace of those old days is combined with the buzz of modern times, the crackle of the wood fire on the hearth as against the hum of the passing cars, familiar covers of one's books lit up by inverted lamps of 100 watt power. What a jolly home it is, and how wonderful it was to be together in it this Christmas. Howard got home on December 21, welcomed by all of us on the dockend in New York, and conveyed by car to Germantown in joyous parade. Christmas was almost an anticlimax and I felt we hardly did it justice although, as usual, it was celebrated with gusto at FJS*[4] *and 704*[5] *(88 present in the evening).*

Since then, life has been busy. Plans for the future are nebulous. The AFSC wants Howard to sign up for a five-year term, as commissioner to visit foreign lands and centers to keep the home office on good terms with foreign friends, a very important task. I do not thrill over the absences, but realize it is the kind of job he would love and, after all, we will need the income to finish the children's education, and so it may be best, certainly far better than being ground to a pulp by the PQ Co.

The American Friends Service Committee decided that Howard would go back to Europe in the summer of 1940. Kitty writes:

Needless to say, we will be desolate without him and my nights of peaceful sleep, all unworried by alarms of overseas cables and sudden phone calls, are rapidly coming to an end. How lovely it has been to have him with us: nice leisurely mornings, shopping, and dining in town, evenings at home by the fire or at the movies, or with friends. Now this six-month gap which will indeed be hard to face without his cheery presence and loving thought for us.

Howard sailed today and I feel as if my heart sailed with him. Poor darling; it was an awful decision to make and took lots of courage.

March 22, 1940

The quiet war in Europe suddenly erupted with a fury. Holland, Belgium and France were overrun. The British managed to evacuate part of their army from Dunkirk with a great loss of men and equipment. In June, France surrendered—a shattered and defeated nation. The threat of warfare hung over Kitty and she worried. Howard's letters indicated his feeling of shut-in-ness with one door after another closing between him and home. He finally managed to leave through Lisbon, after a harrowing trip across occupied France and Spain. He was home in June. Howard was so glad to be home that he didn't mind the overcrowding on the ship. On June 22, 1941, Germany attacked the Soviet Union. *Operation Barbarosa* was supposed to be completed in six months or less.

Kitty and Dody spent a peaceful summer at Pocono Lake while Howard and Peter toured southern and mid-western Quaker Yearly Meetings. Howard gave a series of lectures to interested groups on the situation in Germany and the Quaker service in Europe. Once home, he was off again on more speaking engagements.

Amazing news burst upon us at about 2:00 p.m. as we sat drinking our after dinner coffee, and it was that Japan had bombed Pearl Harbour and Manila, and even the city of Honolulu. All these attacks occurred as two of their wily representatives were in Washington, supposedly negotiating peace. Indeed, they especially asked for two weeks to bring about better terms, and all the while they were slipping across the Pacific, and their airplane carriers were drawing nearer to Hawaii loaded down with bombers.

December 7, 1941

Germany declared war on the United States on December 11, 1941. Kitty had all the usual worries, but she was mainly concerned about her son. He had turned 19 and was subject to the draft. Christmas was celebrated with gay abandon because nobody knew what the next year would bring.

Two and a half years of light and shadow and joy and sorrow had come to a dreadful end, and the whole world was at war. The gray-green soldiers of the Reich occupied all of Europe. The black uniformed Gestapo continued the systematic roundup and extermination of the Jews and other opponents of the Reich. The Holocaust had begun in earnest.

Notes – Chapter 13

[1] This was the last civilian voyage made by the SS *Aquatania*. For the remainder of the war she was used to carry troops between Halifax, Nova Scotia, and the UK. The vessel was decommissioned after the war.

[2] Clarence Pickett was the Secretary of the Philadelphia-based American Friends Service Committee, Howard's employer.

[3] Howard was badly injured in an automobile accident during a German government-sponsored trip to Warschau, while travelling with fellow Quaker representatives Morris and MacDonald.

[4] Francis J. Stokes (FJS), Kitty's uncle, always hosted Christmas dinner for the family.

[5] 704 Locust Avenue was about two miles from *Honey Run*. 704 had been built by Kitty's grandfather Stokes in the 1870's. Kitty's parents rented the house from her great aunt, Hannah Bacon Evans. It remained in the family until 1951.

14

Philadelphia: The War Years

THE house was cold. The oil allotment for the month had run out. Wood fires blazed in the living room and kitchen, but the upstairs was cold, and at times unpleasant. Hot water bottles and the warming pan took the chill off the sheets. The house was still cold.

The United States was at war, with all the accompanying regulations and restrictions. There would be four years of domestic struggle with ration cards and food stamps. There were shortages of everything; only vegetables and fruit were not rationed.

Kitty writes the following 1944 prices in her journal:

Before I forget it, I want to write down a list of some of the things which are rationed, for I know that when the war is over, one would find it difficult to believe we were cut so close.

- *meat of all kinds, except chicken or fish – about 2 lbs a week*
- *fresh fish – 35–80¢/lb*
- *eggs – 70¢/doz.*
- *coffee – 1 lb every five weeks*
- *sugar – 2 lbs a month*

- *butter – ½ lb a month*
- *other fats, oil, and cheese—rationed more than just occasionally and on the same card as meat*
- *canned asparagus – 40¢/can*
- *Fresh fruits and vegetables are not rationed, but are awfully expensive, so one often has to substitute canned goods. For instance: peaches – 23¢/lb; blackberries – 39¢/qt; cantaloupe – 35¢/lb; cherries – 38¢/lb are out of sight; Bartlett pears – 8¢ each; corn, in season – 5¢/ear; cabbage – 14¢/lb; lettuce – 19¢/head.*

One has to go slow on these old favorites and victory gardens will help a lot. Aside from food, it is hard or impossible to get flashlight batteries, any metal cooking equipment, no elastic article, no alarm clocks or radios, no inner spring mattresses, no new telephones. Stores will not deliver packages—milk comes every other day—and so on, ad infinitum.

Just a few of the inconveniences war brings in its train, and yet we are all adaptable folk and we shape our lives to suit and go merrily on our ways—grumbling happily.

Kitty had two households to care for, her own and the home of her elderly parents. Rationing made car travel very difficult (only one-and-one-half gallons of gas were allowed per week). The ration cards could be saved up and used for a special trip. Howard was away a good deal of the time, visiting CPS[1] camps all over the country. Her son had been drafted and assigned at first to a soil conservation camp, then a state mental hospital and finally as a guinea pig for a jaundice research study at Yale. Kitty and her daughter lived at home.

Her Uncle Alfred died:

It seems rather a coincidence that Samuel Mason, the first, was born in 1766 and died in 1842, aged 76, and that his grandson, Alfred C. Mason, was born in 1866 and died in 1942, aged 76—just 100 years between them. I have just come back from Uncle's funeral; a kindly, cheerful and patient spirit has left us in his going. His clothes, returned to us from the hospital, seemed to speak of him by their very shape—large hat, brown suit and well-shined shoes. The little pile seemed pathetic without their owner.

In the spring of 1942, her dear Aunt Edith (Mason) Smith, aged 85, passed away.

Her geniality, her jokes, her blue eyes, and lovely curly white hair, and her love she always showed to her family. She will be sorely missed. She and I were great chums, seeing things often from the same slightly unusual angle, that gave us great pleasure in a slightly cockeyed way—an Irish whimsy perhaps inherited from a bog-trotting ancestor.

In her journals, Kitty comments on the war in Europe and the reports of frequent and widespread destruction. Her heart goes out to the French, but she wonders what has happened to their spirit, which was so evident during the First World War. Although she deplores the bombing, she expresses little sympathy for the Germans, or rather the Nazis, and certainly none for the Gestapo and their extermination camps.

The war in Asia seems quite removed in her journal and her comments reflect this. She shows a strong prejudice against the Japanese, which is strange, as she was not basically a prejudiced woman.

On the home front, the Philadelphia transit strike was a shocker. It was a strike formed along strictly racial lines. Kitty had never really understood the aspirations of the Black population, except that they were there. Now she showed remarkable sympathy toward integration. Why not black motormen and conductors on the trolleys and buses?

Her Quakerism is really tested, for she comments:

The Meeting has turned into a debating society. Friends are more interested in social issues than basic religious beliefs. Maybe we have been too quick to accept people into membership of our beloved society.

This does not reflect her concerns for social issues, but there was a place for such discussions, and Meeting for Worship was not the place.

Much of her thought during these years concerned her daughter. Theodora was a senior at school and preparing for college. She had to take the Scholastic Aptitude tests twice, as she didn't do very well on the first go-round. Kitty didn't really know which direction her daughter would take. There was also a series of boyfriends flowing in and out of her life. These were a worry. Kitty writes:

As for me, I plug along, trying to keep the home fires burning. Apparently, I have reached that period of my life when the mysterious 'change' occurs of which one speaks in baited breath. So far, so good—except that I have dropped from a constant 140 lbs to a pleasant 128 lbs in the past year, without knowing exactly how. Eyeglasses need changing to bifocals for distance seeing—and oh, only a queer, dry sensation in my mouth.

Although she didn't realize it, these signs marked the onset of diabetes and, within a month, she was in Lankenau Hospital. To be diabetic was such a bother. Kitty had always felt that she had a strong heart and that her health was excellent. In her journal, she expresses her incredulity as to how this came about. With the benefit of hindsight, it is obvious that diabetes was an inherited trait. Both her mother and grandmother had the disease, but in the early years of the century, treatment was non-existent. Now she had to be attentive to her diet and blood sugar levels, and give herself insulin shots every day.

The war was drawing to a close. The German armies were in full retreat as the allied armies raced across Europe from east and west. Hitler committed suicide in his bunker on April 30, as the Soviet Army entered a battered and defeated Berlin. The British, Canadian, and American armies liberated Western Europe. De Gaulle and the Free French paraded down the Champs Elysées, and liberated Paris. Slowly, the war was drawing to an end.

Notes – Chapter 14

1 Civilian Public Service (CPS) camps were established by the government for conscientious objectors. The camps were located all over the country.

15

Post-War Philadelphia, 1945–1947

THE greatest and most devastating war in history is over today. The peace, unconditional surrender by Germany, was signed by General Jodl for them at Rheims in the presence of officials of the Allies and press representatives. Philadelphia is taking it very calmly. It is raining and there is to be a gathering at Independence Hall at noon, but I have not heard a single siren or horn and the general feeling seems to be that we have still another war to win in the Pacific and, until that is over, there is no time for celebration. So today, though one is rejoicing, is also a day of sadness for the loss of millions of young fellows all over the world, cut off in their prime and for those yet to be so needlessly sacrificed.

VE Day, May 8, 1945

The next page in her journal is a picture of the Brandenburger Tor, in the heart of Berlin, showing a column of German war prisoners marching down the road. Her comment:

This is the gate through which we drove in little "Immer grade aus" (the name of their car) every morning to work in the Quaker Büro—an office which has been destroyed, as we found out, being in the center of Berlin. What a change since those days of 1938–39.

The 40,000,000 casualties was appalling, and almost too great to comprehend. This did not take into account the casualties in the Pacific or the victims of the Holocaust.

Pete has thrown a bombshell into the family by writing that he has found a girl, Harriet Francke, from Long Island, age 21, a Bucknell College graduate and a wonderful girl as he says.

May 1945

This took a bit of getting used to on Kitty's part, because she had not thought of the possibility of her son marrying and setting up a household of his own. She comments that he had been away from home for five years and would probably not be home again.

Howard was travelling out West.

Dody, Susie, (a boarder) and I dined on Thursday at the Gateway at Reading Terminal, and there was not one meat dish offered out of six main courses on the menu. There was fish (two kinds) crab, mushrooms and a vegetable platter, and some kind of egg affair, but no meat. How wonderful it will be when all this haggling over food will be forgotten.

As for the world war news, my interest has waned, as the little Pacific islands that are taken one by one—at such terrific cost to our men—mean nothing to me, even by name. All I think about is how Tommy Foster, tailgunner in a B-29 bomber, is faring. Pete called up his mother and found he had made 30 missions over Japan proper, from the island base of Tinian and, after five more, he can come home. Oh, that nothing happens in one of those last five trips, and that he gets home safely.

The war against Japan continued with the bombing of the home islands.

Isn't it ghastly to deliberately destroy a country like this—the only hope is that the Japs will sue for peace before everything is wiped out. In Europe, the mess is general. Franco, while visiting Italy, is suggesting that he put Juan Carlos (the last of Alphonso's sons) back on the throne of Spain. In Holland, Queen Wilhelmina suggests that she abdicate in favor of Prince Bernhard, Julianna's husband, very popular though a German. In Belgium, the Parliament has requested Leopold to stay out of the country, and resign his throne. He will do the first, but not the last, he says. In Romania, young King Michael is hand in glove with the Russians and has just received a top decoration for being a "good boy." Still younger King Peter, of Jugoslavia, is not so lucky, as he is still out of the country but has just acquired a son and heir. The Scandinavian rulers, Gustav of Sweden, Haakon of Norway, and Christian of Denmark, are still all in the saddle and apparently popular with their people and, of course, King George VI and Princess Elizabeth (now 19) are more enclosed in English hearts than ever—due to their behavior in the tribulations of this war which they have not run away from.

August 6 was a dramatic day which changed the world. The

United States dropped an atomic bomb on the Japanese city of Hiroshima. Sixty per cent of the city, along with 300,000 people, vanished in a twinkling of an eye. Kitty writes:

> *A horrible future looms for mankind if this element is released to the destruction of mankind—maybe the thought will be so ghastly that it will bring about the outlawing of wars. For us, the editorial about it states a third World War would doubtless ruin the earth and its inhabitants; what fools we mortals are!*

After the United States dropped a second atomic bomb on Nagasaki, the Japanese surrendered.

> *...so the war is over. The combination of destruction with the atomic bomb and its ghastly possibilities, and the attack of the Russians through Manchuria, were too much, and so they (the Japanese) agreed to total surrender, only speculating that they can keep Hirohito, as Emperor—which, thank heaven, the Allies have permitted them.*

Later that month, rationing was lifted, much to Kitty's joy. The joy however, was tempered with sadness, for the thousands of Europeans who faced a coal-less winter, and a scarcity of food.

December heralded not only Christmas, but her son's wedding. Peter and his fiance returned to Long Island to prepare for the wedding. Kitty revisited her own memories of her wedding and honeymoon.

> *The house seems very empty without them and both Pete and I were pretty low just at the last minute when it swept over both of us that he had just spent his last night at home as an*

unattached boy. What a step, when one leaves home like this, for though you come back, it isn't the same. I remember very distinctly coming home from my honeymoon, and walking up Locust Avenue thinking well, we have had a lovely week, Howard and I, at Meadow Farm, *but now he might go home and so would I. Pete will never feel that way I'm sure. I must have been a cool detached sort of person, I think.*

She goes on to say what wonderful times she and Howard had when they were first married and, of course, in the years after.

Peter's wedding, Christmas, her father and mother's sixtieth wedding anniversary and, finally, the announcement that her daughter and Tom Waring were planning to marry in June, all in the space of about one month. It was almost beyond belief that such events could follow so rapidly on the heels of each other.

The year passed quickly. Tom and Pete had returned to college after a three-year interruption. Kitty's first grandchild was born in December: Jane Mason Elkington was named for Kitty's grandmother Jane (Edge) Mason. After every visit to her grandparents, Kitty's father would shyly say, "Please give my love to Jane Mason." His new great granddaughter was very special.

In March, Kitty wrote:

Yearly Meeting is just over and a rather momentous one it was too, as in one of its sessions the motion was made to form a Philadelphia General Meeting of Friends[1] *to include the Hicksites and us. This is a tremendous step after 119 years of separation, and many Friends were much moved thereby. It seems strange that there should, once more, be an Evans in the clerk's seat, as there probably was at the time, or near it, as Harold's great grandfather, my great, great grandfather, Jonathan Evans, had much to do with the separation. And Harold is a splendid clerk, courteous and clever, and yet capable of keeping the reports rolling without making people feel pushed. The weather for the week was perfect, and many spring hats blossomed out in great style. It is always fun to see one's friends, some of whom you only meet at that time; it always gives one a happy feeling with many nice folk. Roots really mean a lot to me, and Philadelphia Quaker roots especially.*

The Philadelphia Quakers were her spiritual foundation and, next to her family, provided a sense of stability and serenity.

Later that Spring, she remarks joyously of seeing an opossum in the yard and that the third generation of hawks were nesting in the trees.

Nineteen forty-seven was a traumatic year, beginning in April when her beloved father died peacefully after slipping into a light comma. At 87 his body just wore out. He had never really been sick, and had always lived a careful, ordered life. He had played golf regularly until he was 85. Now he was gone.

Yesterday evening, at about 7:15 p.m., my darling father very quietly drew his last breath, and left behind him a family in which his going made the first break. One cannot be too sad, however, in losing him, for the last thing one would wish would have been a long illness for a man who had been so active and well all his life and who hardly knew what it was to be sick in bed. . . . So closes the life of a gentleman of the old school, beloved by many for his courtesy, kindness, his dignity, and integrity. I am so glad his grandchildren knew and loved him and that he had pleasure in seeing his first little great granddaughter, Jane Mason Elkington, named for his mother.

As the coffin was being carried out the door, Kitty's mother turned to her and said, " There goes my life." Kitty goes on to say:

And 704 is haunted for me, as each time I open the door, I expect to be greeted by him, or see him sitting in his chair by the fire, smoking and reading—always loving and cordial. Mother is going to look and listen for that step and voice in vain, I'm afraid.

The spring and summer were filled with excitement. Howard was off travelling. Their daughter, Dody, and husband Tom went to Finland to do reconstruction work. Their son and his family drove to Saskatoon to take summer courses at the University of Saskatchewan. Then there was the hectic search for a companion for her mother. That dear lady was slowly and steadily losing her memory. Today we would diagnose this as Alzheimer's disease.

Old age is sad when powers begin to go—and all the more to do. I give thanks for Dad's peaceful passing, although still I can hardly believe he has gone forever, his spirit seems so near and dear.

Later in the summer, she makes the following comments:

We sometimes think that Germantown Avenue is not the quietest place to live, although the new trolleys are a great boon. Well, yesterday we were highly amused on arriving home after a day in the so-called country, to add up the noises we had been subjected to. First, at Sellersville, PA—much traffic, and the scream of a train. Then, through Emaus, PA—the shunting of cars and more engine whoops, (here we had to stop talking) and, as we left, electrically recorded chimes from the church next door, deafening, brazen. At Trexlerville Inn, a jukebox provoked us to move our table. En-route home, a fearful thunderstorm, cracked and snapped, and to cap it all, the fire siren went off over our heads. So we thought we were not so badly off after all when we got back to dear Honey Run *and were enveloped by the peacefulness that awaits one at the opening of the front door.*

A letter from her son said that they had visited with the Doukhobors in Saskatchewan. They represented the fourth and fifth generation of Elkingtons to meet with the Doukhobors.[2]

November came, bringing on the steady deterioration of her mother's health. Her memory was deteriorating and she was becoming more feeble by the day. On November 26, Kitty writes the following sad entry in her journal, for it marked the end of an era.

Who would have thought that my darling mother would have outlived father by just six months, dying this morning very quietly at 11:15, after about three days of comatose condition. It is an awe-inspiring spectacle to watch the oncoming, relentless march of death, stealing away one living part after another until the last faint gasps for air and the last faint flutter of pulse show the passing of the vital spirit within. Mother's gallant fight for life, in the face of much weakness and exhaustion, was remarkable, lasting for two days and nights, during which time one could hardly think she could stand the strain. Yesterday, I think she knew me as her eyes turned when I moved before her; the day before she said little and that very hard to understand, but she did say, 'I see a face in a yellow cloud'—and I wondered whose face she saw—God's or man's. She was such a brave sufferer, never complaining of pain or annoyance, but always with such a sweet smile or a loving 'darling'—even though she was not clear as to who she talked with. A perfect lady, whose mental confusion brought no vulgarity or coarseness to the surface—but one whose subliminal self was restrained by years of pure living and thinking.

Throughout the six years of her paralysis and heart attacks, I have hardly ever seen her be anything but plucky, although she would occasionally sigh and say how disgusted she was with herself to be such a clumsy person. For anyone who had been as active as she, it was a bitter punishment to be dependent on others, and I often felt awful at having to put through things that went against her grain, and to decide things that she would have decided had she been normal. I'm afraid at times she felt crushed and thwarted, and I have often hated myself for apparently being the one who did the thwarting. I hope she forgives me now and understands that I meant to do my best. Bless her sweet blue eyes, how I will miss their dear look, and how empty Locust Avenue will seem now, with both dear ones gone forever.

The year 1947 ended with the closing of a door to the past. The family, which had been such a foundation rock, was no longer there. It struck Kitty that she was now the matriarch of the family and that it was up to her to provide that stability, wisdom, and love for her children and grandchildren[3].

Notes – Chapter 15

1 In the 1820's the *Philadelphia Yearly Meeting of Friends (Quakers)* had split into two groups as a result of theological differences in opinion, centering on the divinity of Christ. They were then known as the *Hicksite* (followers of Elias Hicks) and *Orthodox* (a more conservative, fundamentalist group) branches. For many years, there was little communication between the two groups. Each group held their own meetings and conducted their own business. In 1947, the two branches reunited, forming one *Philadelphia Yearly Meeting*.

2 Joseph S. Elkinton was Howard's grandfather and he had been instrumental in bringing the Doukhobors from Russia to Canada. Joseph S. Elkinton often visited with the Doukhobors, and their children called him "grandfather."

3 Every Christmas night, the Mason, Stokes, and Evans families (up to 120) would gather at 704 Locust Avenue for an evening of song, charades and a general good time. The evening always ended with the singing of *Auld Lang Syne*, a family tradition initiated by Kitty's grandmother in the 1890's, which continued until 1946.

16

Germantown, 1948–1949

For the last week, or so, I have been much occupied with renovation plans for 704. But alas, alack, when one starts down that path, how devious one finds it, and what wheels within wheels one encounters, what yards of judicial red tape. I thought the Nazis had invented red tape! Nothing so simple as just throwing up a few partitions and calling in the plumber and electrician, oh no! Apparently, everyone must have a permit from City Hall before anything can be accomplished and that takes time. At any rate, the zoning must first be changed from residential 'A' to something that permits apartments to be built; and that takes a month.

Philadelphia had long had a reputation as the city that was "corrupt but contented." There had been stirrings of reform, but the entrenched political machine was too strong. The Fire Marshal received regular kickbacks of $10.00 for every oil furnace installed in the city. This he continued to collect, even after indicted and sent to jail. Kickbacks and petty graft were the rule. Kitty had never experienced any of this, because it was always done on the sly between contractors and inspectors. She planned to turn her parents' house into three large apartments. Extensive plumbing and reconstruction needed to be done. She was besieged on every side by the necessity of getting permits for this and permits for that. All along the line, inspectors expected to have their palms greased. The plumber told her that she would have to pay $10.00 extra to the inspector for his cooperation. She absolutely refused to do this, and forbade the plumber to add it to his bill. Subsequently, the inspector stopped the renovation work for some trivial reason. Kitty was furious, and she would have no part in petty graft. She went to the office of the Chief Building Inspector in City Hall, whom she happened to know. She showed him the plans, with which he could find no fault and, as a result, she gained all the required permits. She mentioned the graft. The Chief Building Inspector took her complaint very seriously and assured her that there would be no further trouble. The next day, new and more kindly inspectors came to view the progress of the conversion and approved the work. There was never any mention of Kitty's conversation with the chief building inspector. Kitty didn't know whether the plumber had paid off the inspector or not. But graft was not to be tolerated:

> *Howard calls me one of the 'Proprietors of America' for, as he says, it makes him nervous to learn that women own 70% of all the real estate and do 80% of all the buying. It does seem amusing that here I am, landed with four apartments, one house, one summer camp, and nine garages to care for, all in a rather short space of time; but I find I thoroughly enjoy the job and all that it entails.*

> *April 30 was the first anniversary of dear Dad's burial—how his dignified and affectionate spirit pervades places like 704 and Pocono. Howard and I each felt it up there and spoke of*

how odd it was to feel the place was ours, and not that we were just opening up for them. And now comes Mother's Day, and there is no mother for me to send a present to, and it sweeps over me, all over again—what a vacuum. I wonder if you ever get over missing your mother, your first love? I don't believe you do.

Yesterday, at Horn & Hardarts, *I suddenly heard mother's quiet little chuckle, and turned with joy hoping (oh, how wonderful) to maybe see her dear self then behind me. Who can tell, and maybe she was, but it bruises one's soul not to see her. I think I miss her more all the more as time passes, rather than less; somehow, one feels deserted and lost and kind of alone in the world. Not that Howard isn't a dear, and as good and kind as he can be, but no one can fill a Mother's place, I guess, no matter how old one gets.*

Although life went on, with its crises and challenges, at times Kitty would succumb to tears, though people rarely knew this. The emptiness that she felt was great. In Ellen Berlin's book, *Lace Curtain*, a quotation stuck in Kitty's mind:

It is the passing of the older generation that leaves one lost, not only because their love has been withdrawn, but also because they acted as a bulwark against time, and that withdrawn, leaves you with nothing to hold time back.

This reminded her of something her father said after the death of her Great Aunt Hannah—that he now felt old, having no older generation above him.

These years were perhaps the saddest and loneliest years of Kitty's life. From outward appearances, you would have never known, for she always seemed cheerful and happy. She dearly loved her children and her grandchildren, and had a deep concern for their welfare.

The rest of the year, there were various trips together to visit friends and relatives in Maryland or New England, always returning by way of the summer camp in Pocono. It was here Kitty would relax and gather strength for the coming weeks.

Kitty, a lifelong Democrat, couldn't help chuckling over the Presidential election.[1] Howard was a steadfast Republican, as her own father had been.

> *The biggest political upset for many long years took place today when the Democrats won the election and Truman was returned to the White House by a two million vote majority! A week later, everyone is still gasping, and the pollsters just can't explain it. Of course it is really labor and the farm block that put him in but who would have thought they would have been so united—not Dewey.*[2]

Christmas of 1948 presented a real problem for Kitty. Howard was in Germany until spring. For both her children, it was an "in-law" year, so she was alone. She had never been alone before at Christmas. She sat by the cozy fire in the living room and let her mind go back over Christmases past. It had always been a time of joyous family celebration, but now the family was either dead or scattered. There might be snow, which meant sledding down the back streets, and certainly a bright crisp day— a time for the Mason family to gather, rejoice and reflect on their good fortune. To Kitty, the annual Christmas gathering, full of singing, story-telling, and charades, was the highlight of the year. She remembered her first Christmas gathering when she was ten, and what an occasion it had been. At one end of the dining-room table, a great block of ice, filled to the brim with raw oysters; at the other end, a bowl of Christmas wassail. Now, some 48 years later, she sat by the fire hugging these warm memories to her. There were letters from Howard, but that didn't take the place of his presence.

She closes her journal for 1948:

> *And so I come to the end of my twenty-ninth journal with considerable blessings to think of in the year past.* Honey Run *is a lovely house. As I sit here in our bright, charming living room, with a decorated tree behind me and gifts piled about it, I would wish to say to my great-grandfather (whose journal I have been reading) that I am indeed grateful to the Lord for all his many mercies to me and mine, of which I have often been all too unappreciative. May the coming year find me more thankful and more willing to see the point of view of others and to listen to their opinions. So, my great-grandfather has spoken again after one hundred years of silence.*

Elizabeth Elkington, Kitty's second grandchild, was born on the February 9, 1949. A beautiful little blonde baby weighing 7 lbs. 6 ozs. She lived for just five weeks, but brought joy to all that knew her. Bronchial asthma, followed by a viral influenza, proved too much for her small being.

> *Betsy was buried today under a lovely white blanket of snow, in a grave with her little great-uncle Henry, and her littler aunt and uncle Carol and Christopher. The graveyard was*

beautiful in the softly floating flakes and Howard read from the New Testament *and* The Prophet *and I recited the following few lines which came to me in the middle of the night.*

Go littlest one—but leave us in thy going,
one tender memory of thy baby charms;
So like a bud,
half-opened at break of day unfolding, the morning,
at evening gathered safe in heavenly arms.

As she stood at the graveside, the tender and poignant memories of her own two babies swept over her. Now they were all together, watched over by her parents and grandparents. Tears swelled and it was hard to speak. They left Peter and Franki "to see their baby tucked in."

The summer was filled with great family doings. Her two nieces married and, on June 3, her first grandson, Christopher Gilpin Waring, was born. Later the same month, her son graduated from college. She and Howard were in a daze as this was a day they had looked forward to for so long. Peter had been a reluctant scholar during his school years, but had done very well on his comprehensive examinations. Tom and Dody moved to Denver to start a new career in teaching. Kitty laments that they will be so far away, but feels all will be well.

Two years ago today, my precious mother left us. It seems impossible that two years have gone by, for her dear face and smile are still fresh in my heart as if it were yesterday that we sat together at 704 and talked of the many things that interested her.

November 26, 1949

The first half of the twentieth century is rapidly drawing to a close, and what eventful years they have been. I can hardly enumerate all the major events that have taken place, not the least being two world wars with their frightful results. In a small way, here in the east, we have seen a hopeful upswing in political circles.

The three entrenched, corrupt mayors of Jersey City, Boston and Philadelphia were defeated and their parties turned out of office, much to Kitty's joy.[3]

Christmas was a joy, with eleven family members and friends seated around the table. Kitty was in her element, for she liked nothing better than to have her family around, especially during the holidays. She comments that it never had been so warm as it was on Christmas day: 62°F. Thus, the year ended, full of joy and thanksgiving, and hopes for a peaceful, blessed New Year.

Kitty thanked her Heavenly Father for the blessings of the year past and asked for his guidance for the year ahead.

Notes – Chapter 16

1 Harry S. Truman, Franklin Roosevelt's Vice President, was elected to a full term as President in 1948.

2 Governor Thomas Dewey of New York ran for President in 1948 on the Republican ticket.

3 A great political reform movement swept the country and many of the old, entrenched, and corrupt municipal and state administrations, regardless of their Republican or Democratic leanings, were swept out of office.

17

Germantown, 1950–1954

As the second half of the twentieth century began, Kitty made a decision to take the time to record many of her reminiscences and memories of the previous fifty years.

Beware of all that elusive stuff. Time has a way of slipping by. I want to jot down some of the happenings in the world, this last half-century; events that have made it the most remarkable fifty years in recorded history. I also want to include some of the little things that are not so earth-shattering, yet are so typical of the past years that they are also worthy of recording.

To begin with the year 1900, I had just passed my seventh birthday, and life was very carefree and happy, until the death of Henry in March of that year. This event threw the first of many shadows—of something strange and unexplainable—over our home, and left a great emptiness for me, as he had been a beloved companion and brother. Shortly after this we left the Chew Street house, as the street was being rerouted—under the railroad—and repaved.

We moved to 522 Locust Avenue where we lived until 1917. The family then moved to 704 Locust Avenue where we remained until father and mother's deaths in April and

November of 1947. These early years were lived with great joy and as I look back upon them, only a few unhappy times stand out in my mind.

One of these was the death of Kismet, the darling chestnut horse belonging to Aunt Esther,[1] *whom I had ridden daily for several years, and had driven from the buggy for many years after that. His bright, intelligent face and affectionate ways, had endeared him to us all. He and his brother, Chico, were born in 1886, or thereabouts, and both were raised on Meadow Farm; their mother was a buckskin named Nina. It was a tremendous shock to come back from a trip and be told he was gone; taken away and killed. I remember bursting into tears over the phone and rushing from the room—heartbroken. About three years after this, I was sitting on the porch at 704 reading and, on glancing idly at the stable, what should I see standing under the beech tree, but Kismet swishing his tail back and forth. So clear and distinct was he, that I got up and walked toward him, hoping against hope yet knowing hope was vain. Then he was gone. When I remember how he was during his last year—he would rear back and buck his bridle when hitched—my heart still aches. I felt sure the coachman got drunk and hit him causing his fright—how I hated that man. Yet I never felt quite sure and no one else ever complained or confronted him. Sweet little Kissy, how I loved him, and what wonderful rides we had together.*

Before this first black mark, our afternoons had been spent playing with the Goodhue children (first cousins), at 704. We would play Indians and Whitemen, using the main gates on Locust Avenue and Church Lane as bases, and the whole four acres in between, in which to go scouting. Ev and

I built moss houses under the beeches at 704, tearing up all the moss for roofs and walls, and peopling the mansions with paper doll families. We put on horse shows for Aunt Es who was our audience and offered lots of encouragement. There were Robin Hood plays on the big porch, ever lasting tree houses with perilous aerial approaches, and swacky camp fires over which we cooked unsavory half smokies on sticks. We ate these with great gusto along with tomatoes filched from Robert's garden. We seasoned the tomatoes with rocksalt from the cow shed and handfuls of bran from someplace else.

Some days, simply jumping in the leaf pile or riding the cows or the ever-thrilling game of Kicky Down would satisfy us and we would play around the big barn till we were either chased out by the coachman, or were utterly worn out. Come time to go home, my routine was to jump over the iron bar fence (never walk out the gate) and run as fast as I could to my own gate at 522. I did this in not much more than a minute or two, not arriving in the mood for homework as can be imagined.

School came to an end with graduation at GFS in June 1911. Next year, it was Westtown and what fun that was. In the next three years came a trip to Jamaica, business school, the University of Pennsylvania, Drexel, and the more serious business of getting engaged and married on October 14, 1916.

Since that date, another happy 33 years has elapsed with births and the joy of Peter and Dody to fill them to the brim, as well as sorrows with the coming and going of Carol and Christopher. The aging and deaths of both father and mother also punctuate that happiness and leave their empty places, forever unfilled and unforgotten, and leave me regretting my lack of expressed love, especially in the case of my precious mother.

On the whole, I have been much blessed, and my life has been very happy. Husband and children, and children-in-law, have indeed been great sources of joy and struggle, and now the coming of Janie and Chris add yet more richness to my life.

January 15, 1950

Kitty's third grandchild was born in late March, Judith Elkington, weighing 8 lbs. and 4 ozs.

Life settled into a very comfortable pattern for Howard and Kitty. Up at seven, followed by a cozy breakfast together, either outside on the patio or in the kitchen by the fire. Here, plans for the day were discussed. Howard would be off to work and Kitty would spend the morning doing the household chores. Then lunch and perhaps a nap on the couch in the living room. The afternoon usually centered on some community or Quaker concern. Home to prepare supper. Howard would come bustling in the door, arms full of papers, about 5:30 p.m. A leisurely supper was usually followed by a quiet evening, reading in front of the fire. Howard would retire to his den to write numerous letters and articles. Each of these he would read to Kitty before sending. He would be home for two months, then be off again for another two months, visiting various German groups for the Carl Schurz Foundation. His trips took him all over the country and to Europe. Kitty missed him, but she didn't like travelling the way he did. Meeting groups of people, or staying at strangers' houses was not her thing. While he was away, she would visit family in Maryland, or entertain those members of the family who passed through Germantown. She and sister Evelyn would take trips together, exploring backcountry Pennsylvania or the Eastern Shore of Maryland. They loved to seek out old historical houses, either of Revolutionary or Civil War vintage. She took a keen interest in all her nieces and nephews, as well as her grandchildren.

This pattern continued for a number of years. During the summer months, when Howard was home, they would work in the garden. Howard loved roses and had planted rose trees at the corner of each garden bed. Kitty would work till she was tired and then stop to rest, but Howard worked until he was absolutely exhausted. There was nothing Kitty could do about it, for that was the way he worked. It concerned her a little for they both had turned 60, although both were very healthy. Each worried about the other. They confided their secret worries to their son. Howard's father had died when he was only 61, and this was a concern. So the winter passed uneventfully. Howard did his best to lose weight, but with little success. He still insisted on going to the office every day. Kitty's diabetes was under control. They both looked forward to Howard's retirement when they could spend two weeks together at Pocono.

Philadelphia was undergoing a renaissance.[2] Old slum buildings were being cleared and a new mall had been planned and was being built. This historic park extended from Chestnut Street on the south to Race Street on the north and from Second Street to Sixth Street east and west. Included in the park were the First Bank of United States on Third Street, the Old Customs House on Chestnut Street, two very handsome buildings, Independence Hall and The Quaker Meeting House, at Fourth and Arch, the Free Quaker Meeting House at Sixth and Arch, and finally the Betsy Ross House. The Independence Mall was a concept to engender civic pride. Howard, whose office was in the Old Customs House, had been closely involved with the concept planning and the development of the mall.

News came from Maryland that Kitty's dear Uncle Frank[3] (her golden uncle) had suffered a stroke and was in a coma. This was a shock, for he was the last of the older generation. Together with Uncle Frank, Kitty and Evelyn had planned a trip to Ireland for the fall. Now everything was in limbo. It marked the end of an era. Kitty always knew when the door closed on an era and she remarked on this again and again. There was always some event, which proved to be a marker or a milestone in her life. From now on it would be different. How different she didn't know. At times like these, she gave thanks to her Heavenly Father for the blessings he had bestowed upon her, especially for the people she had known and loved.

Notes – Chapter 17

1 Aunt Esther (nicknamed Aunt Es) was Esther Newlin Stokes, Kitty's aunt, who never married and who died in her early forties.

2 Under the guidance of the National Park Service, historic buildings around Philadelphia's *Independence Hall*, previously neglected for many years, were restored and slums were cleared away to build *Independence Mall* in the center of old Philadelphia.

3 Uncle Frank was Kitty's uncle, Francis J. Stokes.

18

The Journey

You have to walk that lonesome valley,
You have to walk it by yourself.
No one else can walk it for you,
You have to walk it by yourself.

Traditional Kentucky Folk Song

THE leaves were beginning to turn, revealing a spectrum of earthy tones. A cool wind ruffled the lake, and there was a hint of frost in the air. The ferns had turned brown and you could hear the rustling of small animals preparing for their winter's rest. Inside the house a cozy fire was burning; the smoke from the chimney filled the air with its soft sweetness. Kitty sat on the porch of *Hi-Lo Huckleberry*, their house at Pocono Lake Preserve, in one of the big green rocking chairs that had been on the porch of her childhood home. She wore a heavy jacket, for the day was cool but clear—one of those beautiful days of early fall. This would be her last visit to the Pocono cottage for the year. This was her refuge, a retreat from the busy rounds of duties of the city. Here she could refresh her spirit. The wind, the trees, and all the animals, large and small, provided a singular feeling of peace and tranquillity. As she rocked, the words of an old

Kentucky folk song came to her: *You Have to Walk that Lonesome Valley*. Why it had occurred to her then, she didn't know. Perhaps it was something the old Gypsy had said long ago. Lately, her journey had been lonely. Her dearest love was away a great deal, and she missed him. She looked down the path toward the lake and could see the familiar shapes of friends and family that had gone before. Tomorrow, she would close the cottage for the winter and drive back to Germantown.

Kitty's journey had begun so long ago that perhaps even its beginnings were forgotten. Her childhood had been filled with joy, happiness, and some sorrow. Her family was her foundation and her strength. Both parents and grandparents had been an integral part of her childhood. Now there was an emptiness; her father and mother had died and her dear little granddaughter, Elizabeth, had succumbed to a virus when she was just six weeks old. They all were buried together with her own dear babies in the Germantown Meeting burying ground. Purple iris grew around the gravestones. Here was a continuity of spirit.

She didn't know when her journey had really begun. Perhaps it had been the encounter with Gypsies, or maybe the untimely death of her brother Henry from typhoid. Each event had left its mark. She rocked and the little worries and doubts, which are forever on the fringes of our conscience, began to intrude. Had she loved enough, and had she expressed that love to those so dear to her. She hoped so. She and her mother had often disagreed, sometimes over very trivial things. She had loved her father, and he in his own stately way had loved her in return. Her children seemed secure in their own families. Her grandchildren were a constant source of joy. She loved to play games of baseball or tag with them, or read books together. Her grandchildren were all dear to her. But she was alone, walking that lonesome valley. She got up and went inside to make supper. She brought her tray in from the kitchen, put another log on the fire, and sat there enjoying the warmth. Her mind drifted back over her life.

What had she accomplished? What had she done to make the world a better place? She dismissed these thoughts and turned her mind to the things that had to be done in the morning. Tomorrow, she would drive down the mountain to Germantown and *Honey Run*. Her supper finished and dishes washed, the fire dying low and the final chapter of her current book read, she went to bed.

The following morning was bright and clear. She packed the car, locked the doors and drove home. Howard had arrived home and was awaiting her return. What a joy! He didn't look well and she worried. He confessed to shortness of breath and vague pains, which he dismissed as heartburn and indigestion. A visit to the doctor proved nothing substantial, except that Howard was overweight.

In late spring, after a hard day's work in the garden, Howard came in flushed and panting, and sank into his chair complaining of pain in his chest. He was sure it would pass if he rested awhile. He dozed. Kitty noticed how shallow his breathing was, and she was worried. A second trip to the doctor also proved inconclusive. His heart seemed to be all right. His blood pressure was not seriously high; still Kitty worried. In early June, Howard had a heart attack and was ordered to bed and rest. He found sleeping difficult and was only comfortable and free of pain when sitting up in the bedroom rocking chair. Three weeks passed and he progressed nicely, even coming downstairs once a day. Howard attended the dedication of the Independence Mall. It was a blazingly hot day and there had been no shade. Howard came home pale and exhausted, and promptly went to bed. On July 8,

1955, he had a second, fatal heart attack in the early morning, and died in Kitty's arms. She was now alone. It was indeed a lonesome valley that she now had to cross. The ache and the emptiness created by the loss of her true love, was great. They had been married for 39 years: thirty-nine years of pain, sorrow, joy and bliss. Now there was no one with whom to share her thoughts, plans, or experiences. They had been blessed with loving children and beautiful grandchildren. She wrote the following poem of Tennyson's in her journal.

My God, in whom are all the springs of boundless love
and grace unknown.
Hide me beneath thy spreading wings
Till this dark cloud be overblown.

And the stately ships go out
To their haven under the hill
But oh for the touch of a vanished hand,
And the sound of a voice that is still.

She lived just six more years and then, one night as she slept, she too quietly passed over into that world of abiding love and peace, to join her true love, and her two dear children...

Death is only an old door
Set in a garden wall;
On quiet hinges it gives at dusk,
When thrushes call.

Along the lintel are green leaves,
Beyond, the light lies still;

Very weary and willing feet
Go over the sill.

There is nothing to trouble any heart,
Nothing to hurt at all;
Death is only an old door
In a garden wall.

Katharine Wistar (Mason) Elkinton passed quietly through this door on October 10, 1961. She was 68 years old. Her journey on earth was over.

Afterword

THIS has been a difficult book to write, for I was part of it. My mother and I were very close. We often thought alike. In many ways, our lives were parallel. I can truly say that she was one of the two women in my life whom I loved and by whom I was loved unconditionally in return. In the last years of her life, she was lonely, and I did not truly understand or appreciate this until my own true love passed away. I have written this story, much of it never told before, with love, for a very wonderful and remarkable woman. May her grandchildren, and those who remember her, come to know her better through the telling. I am sure everyone who knew Cousin Kitty also have their own memories and stories to tell.

The name Elkinton or Elkington has been used interchangeably throughout this book. The original family name, in England, was Elkington. An ancestor of mine dropped the 'g' in the late 1600's, while the rest of the family retained it. The reason is unclear. My parent's surname was Elkinton (pronounced Elkington). This always caused difficulty. My father attempted to use the original name in the late thirties but found it too complicated to change all his legal papers. Mother was neutral, feeling at home with either spelling. Meanwhile I had reverted to the original spelling of our surname.

Peter W. Elkington
Revelstoke, BC
January 2001